PLAIN AND FANCY

A Musical Comedy

Book by *Joseph Stein*
and
Will Glickman
Music by Albert Hague
Lyrics by Arnold B. Horwitt

SAMUEL FRENCH, INC.
45 West 25th Street   NEW YORK, N.Y. 10010
7623 Sunset Boulevard   HOLLYWOOD 90046
LONDON   *TORONTO*

Amateurs wishing to arrange for the production of PLAIN AND FANCY must make application to SAMUEL FRENCH, INC., at 45 West 25th Street, New York, N.Y. 10010, giving the following particulars:

(1) The name of the town and theatre or hall in which it is proposed to give the production.
(2) The maximum seating capacity of the theatre or hall.
(3) Scale of ticket prices.
(4) The number of performances it is intended to give, and the dates thereof.
(5) Indicate whether you will use an orchestration or simply a piano.

Upon receipt of these particulars SAMUEL FRENCH, INC., will quote terms and availability.

Stock royalty quoted on application to SAMUEL FRENCH, INC., 45 West 25th Street, New York, N.Y. 10010.

For all other rights than those stipulated above, apply to SAMUEL FRENCH, INC., 45 West 25th Street, New York, N.Y. 10010.

An orchestration consisting of:
Piano/conductor's score
Reed I (flute, clarinet, alto saxophone)
Reed II (flute, piccolo, clarinet, alto saxophone)
Reed III (oboe, English horn, clarinet, tenor saxophone)
Reed IV (clarinet, tenor & bass clarinets)
Reed V (bassoon, clarinet, baritone saxophone)
Trumpet I & II
Trumpet III
Horn
Trombone I
Trombone II
Percussion (Timpani, Xylophone, Drums)
Violins A & C (2 books)
Violins B & D (2 books)
Viola
Cello
Bass
Harp

Printed in U.S.A.

ISBN 0 573 68048 5

For Sale:
25 Chorus Books @ $4.00 each

will be loaned two months prior to the production ONLY on receipt of the royalty quoted for all performances, the rental fee and a refundable deposit, The deposit will be refunded on the safe return to SAMUEL FRENCH, INC. of all materials loaned for the production.

PLAIN AND FANCY

STORY OF THE PLAY

(18 males; 11 females; extras)

The story of *Plain and Fancy* is more plain than fancy, as it should be. It concerns a young New Yorker and his sophisticated girl friend who drive down into the Amish country to sell a piece of property he has inherited but has never seen. In this neighborhood of Bird-in-Hand they find themselves out of their metropolitan world, in a land of quaint customs, stern morals and "Pennsylvania Dutch" English. They run across a romance or two among the young generation of Amish, and manage to fix things up so that everybody is in love with the right party at the end—which is how any sensible musical should end.

The following is a copy of the program of the first performance of *Plain and Fancy* as produced at the Winter Garden, New York City, the week beginning January 28th, 1955:

Richard Kollmar and James W. Gardiner

(in association with Yvette Schumer)

Present

PLAIN AND FANCY

A new Musical Comedy with

Richard Derr	Barbara Cook	David Daniels
Shirl Conway	Daniel Nagrin	Stefan Schnabel
Douglas Fletcher Rogers	Gloria Marlowe	Sammy Smith

and Nancy Andrews

Book by Joseph Stein and Will Glickman
Lyrics by Arnold B. Horwitt   Music by Albert Hague
Production directed by Morton Da Costa
Dances and Musical Numbers staged by Helen Tamiris
Sets and Costumes designed by Raoul Pene Dubois
Lighting by Peggy Clark
Orchestrations by Philip J. Lang
Vocal Arrangements by Crane Calder
Musical Director: Franz Allers

CAST

(As they appear)

RUTH WINTERS .... *Shirl Conway*
DAN KING .... *Richard Derr*
A MAN .... *James Schlader*
ANOTHER MAN .... *Herbert Surface*
KATIE YODER .... *Gloria Marlowe*
PAPA YODER .... *Stefan Schnabel*
ISAAC MILLER .... *Sammy Smith*
EMMA MILLER .... *Nancy Andrews*

4

EZRA REBER .... *Douglas Fletcher Rodgers*
HILDA MILLER .... *Barbara Cook*
A YOUNG MILLER .... *Scotty Engel*
ANOTHER YOUNG MILLER .... *Elaine Lynn*
PETER REBER .... *David Daniels*
RACHEL .... *Ethel May Cody*
SAMUEL ZOOK .... *Daniel Nagrin*
LEVI STOLZFUSS .... *William Weslow*
JACOB YODER .... *Will Able*
SAMUEL LAPP .... *Paul Brown*
ABNER ZOOK .... *Edgar Thompson*
IKE PILERSHEIM .... *James S. Moore*
MOSES ZOOK .... *James Schlader*
ABNER ZOOK .... *Tim Worthington*
AN AMISHMAN .... *Herbert Surface*
BESSIE .... *Betty Zollinger*
SARAH .... *Martha Flynn*
ESTHER .... *Cecile Descant*
REBECCA .... *Betty McGuire*
MARY .... *Sara Aman*
STATE TROOPER .... *Ray Hyson*

DANCERS: *Sara Aman, Olga Bergstrom, Cathy Conklin, Andora, Joan Darby, Nina Greer, Reby Howells, Norma Kaiser, Elaine Pallie, Charles Czarney, Jeff Duncan, Eddie Weston, James S. Moore, Hunter Ross, Jimmy Ryan, Robert St. Clair, William Weslow, Don Emmons.*

SINGERS: *Adele Baker, Martha Flynn, Cecile Descant, Jessica Haist, Ellen McCown, Betty McGuire, Faye Winfield, Betty Zollinger, Jimmy Allison, Paul Brown, John Dennis, Ray Hyson, Jack Irwin, Robert Kole, Herbert Surface, Edgar F. Thompson, Tim Worthington, Jim Schlader.*

The play is divided into two acts.

The action takes place in and around Bird-in-Hand, a town in the Amish country of Pennsylvania.

TIME: *The present.*

SCENES

ACT ONE

SCENE 1: *A section of road, outside Lancaster.*
SCENE 2: *Another part of the road.*
SCENE 3: *Another section of road, in One.*
SCENE 4: *The Yoder yard.*

SCENE 5: *The Yoder parlor.*
SCENE 6: *Behind the Yoder house, in One.*
SCENE 7: *Barnyard of the River farm.*
SCENE 8: *A bedroom in the Yoder home.*
SCENE 9: *The Yoder yard.*
SCENE 10: *The Yoder barn.*

ACT TWO

SCENE 1: *The River Farm barnyard.*
SCENE 2: *Kitchen of the Yoder home.*
SCENE 3: *Back porch of the Yoder home.*
SCENE 4: *Bedroom of the Yoder home.*
SCENE 5: *A section of road.*
SCENE 6: *A carnival grounds.*
SCENE 7: *Side porch of the Yoder house.*
SCENE 8: *The Yoder yard.*

MUSICAL NUMBERS

ACT ONE

YOU CAN'T MISS IT—*Richard Derr, Shirley Conway and Ensemble*
IT WONDERS ME—*Gloria Marlowe*
PLENTY OF PENNSYLVANIA—*Nancy Andrews, Douglas Fletcher Rodgers, Elaine Lynn and Ensemble*
YOUNG AND FOOLISH—*David Daniels*
WHY NOT KATIE?—*Douglas Fletcher Rodgers and the Men*
YOUNG AND FOOLISH (Reprise)—*Gloria Marlowe, David Daniels*
BY LANTERN LIGHT—*Danced by Daniel Nagrin and Norma Kaiser with Sara Aman, Elaine Pallie, Nina Greer, Charles Czarney, Jeff Duncan and Bob St. Clair*
IT'S A HELLUVA WAY TO RUN A LOVE AFFAIR—*Shirl Conway*
THIS IS ALL VERY NEW TO ME—*Sung and danced by Barbara Cook, James S. Moore, William Weslow and Ensemble*
PLAIN WE LIVE—*Stefan Schnabel and Ensemble*
THE SHUNNING—*The Company*

ACT TWO

HOW DO YOU RAISE A BARN?—*Stefan Schnabel, Douglas Fletcher Rodgers, Nancy Andrews, Daniel Nagrin and Ensemble*
CITY MOUSE, COUNTRY MOUSE—*Nancy Andrews with Cecile Descant, Ethel May Cody, Betty McGuire, Betty Zollinger, Martha Flynn*
I'LL SHOW HIM!—*Barbara Cook*
CARNIVAL BALLET—*Barbara Cook, Douglas Fletcher Rodgers and Company*

ON THE MIDWAY

MAMBO JOE .... *Daniel Nagrin*
SCRANTON SAL .... *Sara Aman*
ATOMIC LOUIS .... *Eddie Weston*
SAILOR .... *Will Able*
BARKERS .. *James Schlader, Edgar F. Thompson*

DANCE HALL—*the Company*
TAKE YOUR TIME AND TAKE YOUR PICK—*Barbara Cook, Richard Derr, Shirl Conway*
FINALE: PLENTY OF PENNSYLVANIA—*the entire Company*

Plain and Fancy

ACT ONE

SCENE I

Section of road in front of a gasoline station on the outskirts of a small town in Pennsylvania. RUTH *is sitting in a convertible,* DAN *is leaning against a fender, reading a road-map. Pedestrians pass by during scene.*

RUTH. Dan, please ask somebody!

DAN. This is route 27, isn't it!

RUTH. That sign said 27A.

DAN. That's the same as 27.

RUTH. Dan, I feel that "A" is important. Please ask somebody.

DAN. Don't worry, we'll find it.

RUTH. We'll never be heard from again! Dan, why didn't you sell your farm through a real estate agent?

DAN. My grandfather lived on that farm. I want to take a look at it before I sell it. Besides, I figured there might be a story in these Amish. They're fascinating people.

RUTH. You just wrote a story for *Cosmopolitan* on the Pennsylvania Dutch.

DAN. Honey, that was not the Pennsylvania Dutch. It was the Philadelphia Athletics.

RUTH. Dan, I swear we've been on this road before! Please ask somebody!

DAN. All right! I'll ask somebody. *(To* MAN, *entering from Right)* Say, buddy— Can you tell me how to get to Bird-in-Hand?

*(*RUTH *gets out of car.)*

MAN. Where?

DAN. Bird-in-Hand.

MAN. Where's that?

DAN. It's near Ephrata.

MAN. You want Ephrata?

DAN. No. Bird-in-Hand.

MAN. *(Crossing to* RUTH) Boy, you are lost! How'd you get off this road

8

(SONG: "YOU CAN'T MISS IT")

(RUTH, DAN, *and* ENSEMBLE.)

RUTH.

We were doing fine on the Pennsylvania Turnpike
Where the toll-gates and the Howard Johnsons grow:
But we wandered off the Pennsylvania Turnpike—

DAN.

That was several years ago!
We were searching for a little town called Bird-in-Hand,
Near a Pennsylvania county known as Berks.

RUTH.

If there's anybody here who ever heard of Bird-in-Hand,
Will he please for God's sakes tell us where it lurks!

CHILD. *(Spoken)* You've got a road-map, Mister. Cantcha find it on the road-map?

DAN.

On the road-map it's a cinch, my little elf.
What eludes us is the town itself.

MAN 2. Did you say Bird-in-Hand?

RUTH. Yes!

MAN 2. *(Sings)*

It's very simple, lady. I can tell you how to get there.
Past the second traffic light.
You'll see a barn that's big and white:
Take the highway to the right—

ENSEMBLE.

You can't miss it!

MAN 2.

Just keep going till you see,
Near a corner grocery,
There's a road marked 203—

ENSEMBLE.

You can't miss it!

GIRL.

Pretty soon there comes a fork in the road like this.

MAN 2.

Go left then right then left then right—

ENSEMBLE.

It you can't miss.
Then you go straight ahead until you land
By a frozen custard stand—

DAN.

And after that comes Bird-in-Hand?

ENSEMBLE.

You can't miss it!

DAN. *(Spoken)* Did you get all that, Ruth?

RUTH. *(Spoken)* They lost me at the first traffic light. How did that go again?

GIRL 2.

> There's a shortcut no one knows about?
> Down a back road no one uses,
> Past a gate-house no one's livin' in,
> Cross a drawbrige out of order—
> By the long way takes an hour;
> This'll cut off near a third of it—

RUTH.

> And that leads us into Bird-in-Hand?

GIRL 2.

> Bird-in-Hand? I never heard of it!

LADY.

> There's a charming way to get there,
> Through a valley filled with clover.
> General Washington once slept there—
> We may ask him to move over.

MAN 3.

> Would you care to buy a chicken? *(Produces one.)*

GIRL 2.

> Got some lovely old antiques! *(Shows chamber pot.)*

BOY. *(In space-cadet outfit)*

> Please, sir, can I have a lift?

DAN.

> That depends on where you're heading.

BOY.

> I'm heading for the moon!

DAN, RUTH.

> Is it anywhere near Bird-in-Hand?

RUTH. *(Spoken)* Dan, what are we going to do?

DAN. *(Spoken)* I know! Let's ask somebody!

ENSEMBLE.

> When you see there comes a fork in the road like this:
> Go left then right then left then right,
> It you can't miss!
> Then you go straight ahead until you land
> By a frozen custard stand—

(Car starts to move off with DAN *and* RUTH. RUTH *stands up in car.)*

RUTH.

> Stop! Where the hell is Bird-inn-Hand?

ENSEMBLE.

> You can't miss it!
> You can't miss it!

(ALL *look off Right, as car moves off Left, then turn to see where it is going.*)

(*THE MAP SCRIM FLIES IN ON THE DIMOUT, AND SPOT-LIGHT LOCATES BIRD-IN-HAND ON THE MAP.*)

(*AS THE SPOT-LIGHT DIMS OUT, MAP FLIES, REVEALING AN AMISH BUGGY, WITH* KATIE AND PAPA.)

ACT ONE

SCENE II

A country road in an Amish community. The lights reveal PAPA YODER, *Left, and* KATIE, *his daughter, Right, in an Amish buggy.*

KATIE. We're almost home, Papa!

PAPA. Yah! You must be tired from riding, Katie.

KATIE. Not so|

PAPA. *(Looking off)* Is that Ezra in the cabbage field?

KATIE. I don't think so. Maybe Ezra would not be working to-day.

PAPA. Why not?

KATIE. Possible he is getting ready for the wedding.

PAPA. Getting ready? The wedding is not for two days yet. What is there to get ready today?

KATIE. Well, maybe getting his clothes fixed up—maybe taking a bath—

PAPA. Since when does a girl think of a man taking a bath, nokkid?

KATIE. Papa, I did not mean it like that— I meant—

PAPA. I'm sorry already I took you to Lancaster.

KATIE. Papa, just once before a girl gets married, she has a right to go by a big city.

PAPA. A right, she says! A right! Your Mama didn't go to Lancaster 'til she was 48 years old.

KATIE. I know, Papa.

PAPA. A year later, she was dead.

KATIE. Please, Papa.

PAPA. Who knows what germs she caught there!

KATIE. Papa, don't talk so sad. I enjoyed to be in Lancaster. So many people! And everybody talking and laughing!

PAPA. They are foolish people! In all Lancaster they do not even grow a turnip.

KATIE. And all those automobiles shlitzing up and down the streets! Were you ever in an automobile, Papa?

PAPA. Me?

KATIE. I thought maybe sometimes—

PAPA. Your cousin Abel was one time in an automobile—

KATIE. *(She has heard this before)* I know, Papa—

PAPA. Two and a half years later, dead in his grave!

KATIE. Papa, please—

PAPA. It was the gasoline stink! Ate up his lungs—

KATIE. Papa, today just, let's talk about happy things only.

PAPA. Yah! Ezra is a good man for you, Katie—a good farmer—And it's a fine piece of land I'm buying for him.

KATIE. It will be nice, Papa, ain't?—You on one farm, us on the farm right next. Later some day, it will be one big farm.

PAPA. Some day ain't yet. I ain't dead already!

KATIE. I didn't mean it that way, Papa. I meant—

PAPA. I know, Katie, I know— I wish you could see how happy you look!

KATIE. I am happy! It was such a day!

(SONG: "IT WONDERS ME"—KATIE AND ENSEMBLE.)

KATIE.

It wonders me,
It wonders me,
So beautiful a day can be,
So green the field,
So blue the sky,
So red and gold the maple tree.
Somewhere a breeze begins to sing,
Somewhere a bird is answering;
So wonderful sweet the melody,
It wonders me!

(Music continues, as SIX GIRLS and FOUR BOYS enter in back, seen in silhouette, carrying baskets, rakes, etc.)

So green the field,
So blue the sky,
So gold the tree,
It wonders me!

PAPA. *(As music continues, under)* Before a wedding, it is right for a girl to be happy—

KATIE. *(Taking off her bonnet, revealing prayer cap)* Yah, Papa.

PAPA. It will be nice, Katie, ain't?

KATIE. I hope. I want it to be nice. Like today is nice.

CHORUS.

> It wonders me,
> It wonders me,
> So beautiful a day can be!

KATIE.

> So green the field,
> So blue the sky,
> So red and gold the maple tree!

CHORUS.

> Somewhere a breeze begins to sing—

KATIE *and* CHORUS.

> Somewhere a bird is answering.
> So wonderful sweet the melody,
> It wonders me!
> So green the field,
> So blue the sky,
> So gold the tree,
> It wonders me!

(THE TREE-TRAVELLER CLOSES FROM THE LEFT, DAN
AND RUTH *FOLLOWING IT ON. A BENCH IS SET
DOWN LEFT DURING THE DIMOUT.)*

ACT ONE

SCENE III

*Another section of the road. Played in one, before the Landscape
Tree-Traveller. Bench is Left.* DAN *enters from Left, followed
by* RUTH.

RUTH. *(Following* DAN, *tired)* Dan, you should have asked
somebody.

DAN. *(Has crossed to Right, looking off)* I'm sure it's on this
road somewhere. *(Crosses in to Left Center)* Come on, let's get
back to the car.

RUTH. Relax! *(Sits on bench, takes off shoe and rubs foot)*
We've been in that car for days! What have you got against asking
somebody?

DAN. Who? In the last hour we've passed three pigs and a mail
truck!

RUTH. Who gets mail around here? Do the pigs write to each
other?

DAN. *(Crossing* RUTH, *and looking off Left)* Don't worry, we'll
find it. I bet we're practically on their doorstep.

RUTH. Well, at least we can have a drink. Dan, I've got a bottle
of Scotch in my hatbox.

DAN. *(Good-naturedly, turns quickly to* RUTH) You'd better keep that bottle out of sight. The Amish are against drinking.

RUTH. Oh fine, two days of buttermilk on the rocks! Why didn't you sell your property to that paper box outfit?

DAN. I couldn't do that to these people.

RUTH. They're against paper boxes, too?

DAN. A factory, Ruth— It would bring in thousands of strangers. The Amish want to be left alone.

RUTH. Good idea! *(She rises)* Let's leave them alone and go back to New York.

DAN. You'll really enjoy meeting these people, Ruth.

(RUTH *slowly sits again.)*

Just think of it— They have had practically no contact with the outside world since they settled here in Lancaster County, and their customs haven't changed in all these two hundred years. It's inspiring in a way. The whole world changes around them, but they stand solid with their simple, honest values.

RUTH. Dan, that's beautiful. Dull—but beautiful!

DAN. *(Sitting on bench, Left of* RUTH) No, they're really fascinating. Did I tell you about the buttons?

RUTH. Buttons? What buttons?

DAN. The Amish! They don't use buttons.

RUTH. How do they keep things closed? *(Sees* ISAAC *approaching, offstage Left)* Dan, look—a people, a person—

(ISAAC *enters, with market basket of groceries, crosses them to Right Center.)*

Come on. *(She rises)* I want to see if it's true about the buttons.

DAN. Ruth, please— *(Rises quickly, crosses* RUTH *to* ISAAC) Er —Mister—sir—maybe you can help us—

ISAAC. Yah?

DAN. We're looking for a family by the name of Yoder.

ISAAC. Yoder?

DAN. Yes. Do you know of a family by that name around here?

ISAAC. Yoder? There's maybe fourteen Yoder families.

DAN. I mean on this road.

ISAAC. I mean on this road.

DAN. We're looking for a Jacob Yoder. Is there a Jacob Yoder?

ISAAC. Sure.

DAN. Where can I find him?

ISAAC. Which one?

DAN. Is there more than one Jacob Yoder?

ISAAC. Four of them anyhow.

RUTH. *(To* DAN) Let's get out of here.

DAN. Ruth, wait a minute. *(To* ISAAC) I have a letter here from Jacob Yoder.

ISAAC. Yah. *(Studies letter)* This is not from Fat Jacob Yoder over by Daisy Creek.

DAN. No?

ISAAC. He can't write.

RUTH. Three Jacob Yoders to go.

ISAAC. *(Crossing* DAN *to* RUTH) Maybe could it be Hairy Jacob Yoder with the two fingers missing? *(Gestures two center fingers missing.)*

RUTH. Oh my God. I hope not! How is it there are so many Yoders around here?

ISAAC. Funny, ain't? But not so funny like Zook.

RUTH. What's a Zook?

ISAAC. Also families like Yoder, only more. We got twenty-four families Zook.

DAN. Look, this Jacob Yoder has a daughter.

ISAAC. I know.

DAN. How do you know?

ISAAC. They all got daughters.

DAN. Oh?

ISAAC. Even the one who can't write.

DAN. Well, I understand this daughter is getting married soon.

ISAAC. Oh—Katie Yoder! That Jacob Yoder you're looking for?

DAN. I guess so.

ISAAC. *(Crossing back to Right, picks up his market basket)* He's my brother-in-law. Him you'll find down the road a piece. A house with an elm tree in front.

DAN. Thank you.

(ISAAC *starts to exit Right.*)

RUTH. *(Crossing* DAN, *to Right)* By the way, what's that thing painted on that barn over there, a hex sign?

ISAAC. A hex?

RUTH. Well, I heard that around here, among the Pennsylvania Dutch—

ISAAC. *(Coldly)* That ain't a hex. *(He exits, Left.)*

DAN. Come on, Ruth! *(He crosses to Left.)*

RUTH. *(Crossing to bench, gets handbag)* What's the matter? What did I do now?

DAN. Did you have to mention hex? They don't like to discuss it with outsiders.

RUTH. *(Crossing to extreme Left)* I'm sorry, but how would I know? I'm a Baptist! We have no secrets from anyone!

DAN. Come on—let's get back to the car.

(BLACKOUT. THE LIGHTS COME UP BEHIND THE TRAVELLER, REVEALING A FROZEN PICTURE OF PREPARATION FOR THE WEDDING, THROUGH THE SCRIM. THE TRAVELLER OPENS TO RIGHT ON A MUSIC CUE, AND THE PICTURE MELTS INTO AN ANIMATED SCENE OF APPLE-BUTTER MAKING.)

ACT ONE

SCENE IV

The Yoder yard. The house is Stage Right. FOUR GIRLS are seated on a bench, peeling potatoes in front of it. TWO MEN are sawing firewood with a bucksaw near them. MORE GIRLS are embroidering a tablecloth, up Center. Flowers are being potted up Left Center. Apple butter is being churned down Center. Left Center, there is a wagon, and on it MEN, including EZRA, are displaying vegetables. In front of them, on a crate, GIRLS and RACHEL are peeling apples for the churn. Stage Center, EMMA is fitting KATIE'S dress, as the picture melts into life.

RACHEL. *(On bench, down Left)* Emma, I have here some more apples.

EMMA. Good! *(Adjusts KATIE's apron)* It fits wonderful good, Katie. Ezra, what do you think of your beautiful bride.

EZRA. *(On wagon, holds bushel basket of tomatoes under one arm, single specimen in other hand)* Look at the tomatoes! Big, like pumpkins!

EMMA. Ezra, look at Katie once! Forget the tomatoes!

EZRA. Such tomatoes I can't forget! Look, Samuel— *(He shows them to SAMUEL, who is downstage of the wagon.)*

AMISHMAN 1. Emma, is there enough apple butter?

EMMA. I think there is enough of everything. What a beautiful time of year for a wedding!

(SONG: "PLENTY OF PENNSYLVANIA." EMMA, YOUNG MILLER GIRL, AND ENSEMBLE.)

EMMA.

> Winter is a good time,
> Quieter than some;
> You sit around the kitchen
> And wait for Spring to come.

(KATIE exits into house.)

MILLER CHILDREN.

> Chew your thumb, and wait for Springtime.

EMMA.

> Spring is a good time,
> Lilacs at the door—
> Roses climbing up a garden wall!
> Summer is a good time,
> Time for things to grow,

CHORUS.

> Time for getting ready
> For the very best time of all—

EMMA.

> The Fall!
> Nights are crisp and the air like wine,
> And the leaves begin to burn;
> And the dumbest Dutchman's doing fine—
> Cause—wherever you look,
> Wherever you turn is—
>
> Plenty of Pennsylvania.
> You've never seen the likes of
> Plenty of Pennsylvania,
> Where anything grows!
>
> Plenty of Pennsylvania!
> No pastures green the likes of
> Plenty of Pennsylvania,
> Where anything grows!
>
> All you need is some seed
> And a plow or two
> And a bull who's keeping company
> With a cow or two.
>
> Soon you've got
> Plenty of Pennsylvania:
> Sweet land of meadows golden,
> And fat red barns for holdin'
> What goes to town on market day!
> Plenty of—
> Plenty of Pennsylvan-i-ay!

GIRLS QUARTET.

> Anything grows in Pennsylvania,
> Look around and you can see.
> Anything grows in Pennsylvania,
> Anything and everything, from A to Z!

BOYS QUARTET.

> Anything and everything from A to Z!

(MILLER BOY *helps* GIRL *on to crate, Stage Left.*)

MILLER GIRL.

> Asparagus, broccoli, cauliflower
> Dandelion greens, and escarole,
> Fennel and grapes and honeydew melon,
> *(Prompted by* MILLER BOY)
> And iceberg lettuce for the salad bowl!

CHORUS.
> And iceberg lettuce for the salad bowl!

MILLER GIRL.
> Juniper, kale, and lovely lentils;
> Mushrooms, nutmeg, okra, peas,
> Quinces, rutabagas, squash, tomatoes

(Pause)
> Un-i-ons sweet like strawberries!

(CHORUS *react.*)
> Vinegar—also watermelon,
> X-plants planted all in rows.
> Yams and—zpinach?

CHORUS.
> No!

MILLER GIRL.
> Zauerkraut?

CHORUS.
> No!

MILLER GIRL.
> Zucchini!

ALL.
> In Pennsylvania anything grows!

(REPEAT CHORUS TO FINISH.)

AMISHMAN 2. *(On music break-up)* Do we have enough chairs?
AMISHMAN. 3. Yah! Ezra is bringing more later.
AMISHMAN 4. If you need more, we have plenty at home.

(AMISHMAN 2 *nods, exits Right, below house.)*

AMISH GIRL 1. I hope Bessie brought enough dishes.
AMISH GIRL 2. I think so.
AMISH GIRL 1. Good! Then we'll have enough. *(She crosses up and onto porch, with* AMISH GIRL 3.)

(AMISH GIRL 2 *exits down Right with* EMMA. DAN *and* RUTH *enter up Left, as* HILDA *comes from house, and gathers up the* TWO CHILDREN *and comes down Right.)*

DAN. *(Approaching a group of* AMISH, *down Left)* I beg your pardon—does a Mr. Yoder live here?
> *(They turn to each other in confusion.)*
(DAN *turns to an* AMISHMAN *and* WOMAN *Center)* We're looking for a Mr. Jacob Yoder—

(The AMISH *retreat upstage.)*

RUTH. *(Giving it all up)* Well! It's been a lovely visit! Come on, Dan. *(She starts out, whence they have come.)*

DAN. *(Seeing* HILDA, *with the* CHILDREN*)* Wait a minute, Ruth—

HILDA. *(Steps forward. About 22, attractive, she has a more self-confident manner than the* OTHERS. *At Right Center, with the* CHILDREN*)* You want Jacob Yoder?

DAN. That's right.

HILDA. He lives by here. *(Gestures to house.)*

DAN. Oh. Are you Mrs. Yoder?

HILDA. *(Attracted, and amused)* No, I'm not yet anybody's missus. I am his niece, Hilda Miller. *(Producing the* GIRL*)* This is my sister— *(Pushing* BOY *forward)* And my brother—

DAN. How do you do?

(The CHILDREN *hastily retreat, upstage.)*

*(*DAN *looks around)* Well, I'm sorry if we've interrupted a party or something—

HILDA. *(Looking at him with real interest)* Yah—

DAN. Perhaps we'd better come back some other time—

HILDA. *(Quickly)* No— Stay once.

RUTH. If you're sure we're not in the way—

HILDA. No, no. *(Crosses to* RUTH, *indicating hat)* Pardon me, please—are you a Spanish lady?

RUTH. Spanish—?

HILDA. In a magazine once, I saw a Spanish lady wearing such a thing.

RUTH. *(Realizing that her hat looks exotic)* Spanish? Honey, I bought this at Ohrbach's.

HILDA. *(Bewildered)* Oh— *(Turns to* DAN, *puzzled)* You ain't a farmer, yet.

DAN. *(Amused)* No, I'm not.

HILDA. *(Studies him a moment, to herself)* Golly, what a kind!

RUTH. *(Dryly)* Yes—

DAN. Miss Miller, could you tell Mr. Yoder we're here?

*(*HILDA *starts to exit down Right.)*

I'm Dan King. We just drove down from New York. *(He crosses to Left of* HILDA.)*

(There is a rustle from the GROUP. TWO MEN *cross to below the house.)*

HILDA. *(Stopping)* From New York, all the way to Bird-in-Hand?

RUTH. *(Crossing to Left of* DAN*)* With a torn road map yet! *(Catching herself, to* DAN*)* Yet? Hey, it's catching!

HILDA. *(To* DAN*)* You're the fellow from the River Farm, then.

(The AMISH *react.)*

DAN. That's right.

HILDA. I didn't know such a fellow like you owned it.

DAN. Why? What sort of fellow did you expect?

HILDA. *(Slightly flustered)* I thought an old—I mean—not so fancy— Uncle Jacob is by the barn. Come in the house, once. *(She goes into house.)*

DAN. Thank you. *(He follows her into house.)*

RUTH. *(Starts to follow, looks back, and notices all the* AMISH *staring at her. She smiles at them reassuringly)* No buttons! *(She slides side zipper of her skirt down and up)* See? Zipper! *(She exits into house.)*

(A murmur of amazement wells up among the AMISH.)*

AMISHMAN 3. Did you see their car?

AMISHMAN 5. Without a top, even!

AMISH WOMAN. Did you see the shoes she was wearing?

EMMA. *(Entering from the house)* Who was that Mexican lady?

*(*PETER *enters from Right, crosses to Left Center.)*

AMISH GIRL. Come, bring in the corn—

AMISHMAN 5. Bessie, you bring the tomatoes and I'll bring the—

(The ad libs stops, as they ALL *notice* PETER.)*

PETER. *(To* AMISH WOMAN*)* Hello, Rachel!

RACHEL. *(Warmly)* You look nice, Peter.

*(*EMMA *starts to cross down Center.)*

You fixed yourself by your Aunt. A little fatter.

PETER. Two years with Aunt Anna's cooking, why not?

EMMA. Peter!

PETER. Hello, Emma—busy here.

EMMA. Everybody's bringing for your brother's wedding.

PETER. *(To group down Left)* Oh!—Where's Katie?

*(*EMMA, *concerned, starts to leave.)*

SAMUEL. *(Crossing to Left of* PETER *from* GROUP *down Left)* Hello, Peter, you came back!

PETER. *(Shaking hands)* Hello, Samuel.

SAMUEL. What a nice surprise!

PETER. Yah. Is Katie around?

*(*EMMA *stops, comes back to* PETER.)*

SAMUEL. I guess. You were by the tobacco sale in Lebanon?

PETER. Yah. *(To* EMMA*)* Where's Katie?

EMMA. *(Right of* PETER*)* Peter, Katie is getting married.

PETER. I know.

EMMA. Don't make trouble.

PETER. *(Crosses to* EMMA*)* I only want to talk with her.

EMMA. Once you already got in trouble fighting about Katie. Again you want they should make you go away from here? Don't make trouble.

(A pause. PETER *starts to leave, crossing to down Left.* KATIE *enters from house, sees him.)*

KATIE. *(On porch)* Peter!

PETER. Hello, Katie.

KATIE. I heard you came back.

PETER. *(Crossing up)* Yah. This morning.

SAMUEL. *(Encouraging* GROUP *to leave* KATIE *and* PETER *alone)* Time for supper once, ain't? *(Gives* PETER *a reassuring pat, exits, Right 2 entrance.)*

RACHEL. *(Also going off Right)* Yah. Go wash.

(An AMISHMAN *takes down Left crate off Left, with bowls and fruit.* OTHERS *exit.)*

KATIE. You look nice. A little thinner.

PETER. *(Crossing up Center)* It was hard work by my uncle.

KATIE. *(Coming from porch, crosses to* PETER*)* They are all right, the family there?

PETER. The same. You look nice, too, Katie. *(Steps in)* Like always.

KATIE. Thank you.

PETER. Are you happy, Katie?

KATIE. *(Uneasily)* Yah. Sure.

PETER. Are you happy that you are getting married to Ezra?

KATIE. You know, Peter, today I was by Lancaster.

PETER. *(Unheeding)* I heard only yesterday about you and Ezra. I was surprised. I hardly believed it.

KATIE. I have to go back inside— *(She crosses onto porch.)*

PETER. *(Following)* Where is the promise we made—when we were children, yet?

KATIE. We were so young, Peter. And you were away a long time.

PETER. I do not believe you forgot about us.

KATIE. *(Placating)* I came to an age for marrying. And Papa—

PETER. *(Crossing to below table, Right Center)* Your Papa always liked Ezra. A good farmer—

KATIE. *(Factually)* Yah, he is a good farmer.

PETER. And your Papa would never pick me for his Katie. Peter is a troublemaker—a man who fights, even.

KATIE. Please! Peter—

PETER. *(Crossing to Left of porch steps)* I fought only to keep Amos Beiler's hands off you!

KATIE. I know.

PETER. But your father did not care why.

KATIE. It's no use to talk about it now—

PETER. Your father never cared why about anything. *(He sits on the porch steps)* He saw me when I was plowing once, throw a stone in the river. I told him I wanted to watch the ripples, only. He thought I was a crazy man. He heard me whistle, once, and he told me to my face, "A man who whistles has an empty head!" This is not a man for his Katie.

KATIE. Peter, will you come to my wedding?

PETER. No. *(He crosses away from* KATIE, *to wagon)* It would not make it happier if I came.

*(*KATIE *crosses in to Center.)*

I do not even have a proper present for you.

KATIE. Please—please come.

PETER. Remember the first present I gave you?

KATIE. *(Crossing to* PETER) Yes—

PETER. When you started in school—your first writing book.

KATIE. And you drew a bluebird on the cover.

PETER. With both eyes on one side of his head.

KATIE. Still I have it.

(They exchange a look.)

PETER. It was a silly thing—
  (MUSIC intro for number.)
at that age, to fall in love—

KATIE. Yes—it was.

PETER. *(Rising)* But still you have it.

*(SONG: "YOUNG AND FOOLISH"—*PETER.)

VERSE.
        Once we were foolish children,
        Playing as children play:
        Racing through a meadow, April bright—
*(*PETER *crosses down Left Center, taking* KATIE *with him. She stands below and Right of him, so he can sing front.)*
        Dreaming on a hilltop half the night.
        Now that we're growing older,
        We have no time to play.
        Now that we're growing wiser,
        We are not wise enough to stay—

(They touch, and KATIE *moves a step away, Right.)*

REFRAIN.

> Young and foolish,
> Why is it wrong to be
> Young and foolish?
> We haven't long to be.
> Soon enough the carefree days,
> The sunlit days go by;
> Soon enough the bluebird has to fly.
> We were foolish.
> One day we fell in love;
> Now we wonder
> What we were dreaming of,
> Smiling in the sunlight,
> Laughing in the rain.
> I wish that we were young and foolish again!

(KATIE *is almost moved to kiss* PETER. *MUSIC continues, under.
Bird-Traveller closes.*)

KATIE. *(In torment)* No, Peter— *(Rushes off, down Right)* No!
PETER. *(Sings last section)*

> Smiling in the sunlight,
> Laughing in the rain,
> I wish that we were young and foolish again!

(*After last note, Bird-Traveller opens on the Yoder parlor.*)

ACT ONE

SCENE V

*The Yoder parlor. It is stiffly furnished, seldom used, very clean
and austere. There are doors Right and Left.*

(DAN *is seated at the Left end of a long settle in the middle of the
room, reading Jacob Yoder's letter.* RUTH *is at the Right end
of the same settle.* HILDA *is sitting on a chair, Right of the
settle.* HILDA *looks at* RUTH, *beginning with the feet, finally
catching her eye.* RUTH, *made uncomfortable by this searching examination, clears her throat, attracting* DAN'S *attention.*)

DAN. I hope Mr. Yoder won't be tied up much longer. *(He puts
letter away in pocket.)*
HILDA. Tied up?
DAN. Busy. In the barn, with whatever he's doing.
HILDA. Oh, no. The new calf was yarrixing, and he is taking
care.

RUTH. *(With polite interest)* Yarrixing?
HILDA. *(Frankly)* Vomiting.

(RUTH *looks slightly ill.* PAPA YODER *and* ISAAC *enter Left.* PAPA *stays Left of* DAN. ISAAC *crosses above settle to between* RUTH *and* HILDA, *Right Center.)*

PAPA. Excuse me you're waiting till now.
DAN. *(As* RUTH *rises)* That's quite all right, Mr. Yoder. I'm Dan King.
PAPA. Hello.
DAN. And this is Miss Winters.
RUTH. How do you do?
PAPA. How do you do? *(Gesturing at* ISAAC) My brother-in-law.
RUTH. *(She turns, looks over his head, then finds him)* Oh. Didn't we talk to you on the road?
ISAAC. Yah. Coming from the store I was. They were coming from Ephrata, and—
PAPA. *(Interrupting)* Yah. *(Crossing in between* DAN *and* RUTH) I was busy by the barn. The new calf today all day was yarrixing.
DAN. Yes, we heard the news.
   (RUTH *sits, obviously having had enough of yarrixing.)*
Mr. Yoder, you wrote me about buying my farm—
PAPA. Yah.
DAN. Well, as I was telling Miss Winters, I wanted to take a look at the place before I sold it.
PAPA. *Miss* Winters? *(To* RUTH) You're not married?
RUTH. No, we're not.
PAPA. And you drove all the way here from New York together?
DAN. *(Bewildered)* That's right.
PAPA. *(Condemning them)* Yah! You're going back to New York today?
DAN. We hadn't planned to—it's a bit of a trip. Is there a hotel near here?
PAPA. You came to sell the farm, ain't?
DAN. Yes—
PAPA. By us, people who visit don't go by a hotel. Stay here.
DAN. Oh, no—we don't want to impose—
PAPA. No, there is for you a nice big bedroom in the back. *(To* RUTH) You sleep in the little room under the stairs.
RUTH. The little room under the stairs— *(Rises)* Dan, why don't we go to a hotel? I'd love a hot tub, and—
PAPA. A hot tub you can have here.
DAN. *(Gesturing* RUTH *to be patient)* Just overnight, Ruth. Is my farm far from here, Mr. Yoder?
PAPA. It is right past by my fence over by the river. With the big white barn.

(The Two Miller Children *enter excitedly from Left.)*

Miller Boy. Uncle—
Papa. What?
Miller Boy. The calf—he's again ·yarrixing.
Papa. Ach— I'll be a few minutes only.

(Papa *exits Left, following* Children.)

Isaac. Mr. King, you got a good piece of land. He's buying it for his new son-in-law soon.
Dan. *(Sitting on settle)* So I understand.
Isaac. *(Sighs)* By some people, the daughter gets married, and by some people, not. *(He looks at* Hilda.)
Hilda. *(Embarrassed)* Papa—
Isaac. *(Indicating* Hilda) By her is a foolishness. Men come around by her plenty, but stay they don't.

(Hilda *grimaces. This is an old story to her.)*

Dan. *(Slightly embarrassed)* Well, I wouldn't worry about it, Mr. Miller.
Isaac. She needs marrying. Twenty-two years, yet. Children she should have now. But if there is no man, from where is the children? *(He stares directly at* Ruth.)
Ruth. *(Since it is up to her)* —A good question!
Isaac. *(To* Hilda) See? Even her, she says it.
Dan. Oh, I'm sure she'll get married, Mr. Miller—an attractive girl like Hilda.

(Hilda *smiles, pleased.)*

Isaac. *(Crossing* Ruth *to* Dan) Moses Beiler wanted marrying.
Dan. He did?
Isaac. Hot for her he was. But with her big mouth, she told him straight he is dumb like a cow.
Hilda. Moses Beiler *is* dumb like a cow.
Isaac. *(Enraged, crossing to* Hilda) So? So, you had to tell him?
Hilda. *(Placidly)* Everybody knows. He should know too, ain't?
Dan. Look, Mr. Miller—
Isaac. *(To* Dan *and* Ruth) And Jonas Fisher! A big wonderful built man! With ten acres of tobacco yet! He took her for rides in his buggy. All of a sudden is gefinished! *(Rhetorically)* Why?
Hilda. *(Looking straight ahead)* Jonas Fisher sweats too much.
Isaac. *(Furious)* Every man sweats!
Hilda. Not like Jonas Fisher.
Isaac. *(At his wits' end)* And this she *told* him.

HILDA. *(Demurely)* Papa, you want me to be honest, ain't?

ISAAC. *(Exasperated)* It is also honest not to be a blabbermaul! *(To* DAN*)* Excuse me that I holler, but with Hilda it boils me up. We don't see no man for her!

(The last is to RUTH, *who turns to* DAN *for help.)*

DAN. *(Rises, uncomfortably)* Yes! Well—er—if we're staying, I'll go out to the car and get our bags. Excuse me.

(He is about to leave when KATIE *and* PAPA *enter from Left.)*

ISAAC. This is Katie. For her is the wedding.

RUTH. Well! Congratulations, Katie!

KATIE. *(Crossing to Center, below settle)* Thank you.

DAN. Mine too, Miss Yoder.

(She acknowledges with a shy nod.)

PAPA. *(Crosses to Left of* KATIE, *proudly)* From New York they are. From him I'm buying for you and Ezra the River Farm.

KATIE. *(Sits on settle)* Yes, Papa.

DAN. I'll bring the bags in.

RUTH. Be careful with the hat box! *(Significantly)* Don't drop it!

*(*DAN *goes, after giving* RUTH *the high-sign to drop the subject.)*

ISAAC. *(Looking at* RUTH's *hat)* Excuse me for asking—

RUTH. Yes?

ISAAC. Are you maybe a gypsy lady?

RUTH. No, Mr. Miller. I bought this at a place in New York—

PETER. *(Enters from Left, in agitation)* Mr. Yoder.

*(*ISAAC *moves to above the settle.)*

PAPA. *(Turning)* What are you doing here in my house?

PETER. Mr. Yoder, I want to talk with you.

PAPA. *(Coldly)* About what?

PETER. *(Looks at* OTHERS*)* Alone I would like to talk with you.

KATIE. Peter— *(She starts to cross to him.)*

PAPA. *(Holds her back)* We have nothing to talk. Go out of this house!

PETER. Mr. Yoder, you must listen to me once—

PAPA. Wherever you go comes trouble. *(Sharply)* I want you out of my house!

(PETER *looks at* PAPA *for a moment, and exits Left.* KATIE *crosses* PAPA, *following* PETER.)
(Stopping her with his voice) Katie! You and Hilda go and red up the rooms for the company.

(KATIE *hesitates, then goes obediently, above settle and out Right.* HILDA *accompanies her, her arm around* KATIE.)
Isaac, come help me with the calf. *(He goes, Left.)*

ISAAC. Yah! *(To* RUTH) Miss, you wont to come see the sick calf?

RUTH. *(Rises)* No, thank you, but give him my best.

(ISAAC *starts out Left, as* SIX AMISHMEN *troop in and line up below the settle. They are stolid, heavy-set, some with beards. Their attention is immediately rivetted on* RUTH.)

ISAAC. Ah, look who came around once! Hello!

JACOB. *(The last one in)* We left the pots and dishes in the kitchen. Anything more we can help?

ISAAC. The fixings are all, but stay a little.

(*They* ALL *look to* JACOB *for a decision.*)

JACOB. All right. A little.

ISAAC. We have with us this lady from New York—er—Miss—

RUTH. Ruth Winters.

ISAAC. Make the acquaintance of some friends here. Wonderful live fellows. *(He goes down the line toward Left, introducing them)* Abner Zook—Samuel Lapp—Ike Pilersheim—Moses Zook —Abner Zook—and Jacob Yoder. *(Winking)* Nice fellows! *(He goes out, Left.)*

RUTH. *(Recognizes the last name)* Jacob— Oh! How do you do?

(RUTH *and the* MEN *and left standing, uncomfortably. After a moment she sits. They remain standing.)*
(RUTH *waves vaguely)* Sit down, gentlemen!

JACOB. *(As the* OTHERS *look to him)* We only stay a little.

RUTH. Yes—well— *(Sitting alone is awkward, and she rises)* I'm only staying a little myself. *(There is a huge gap in the conversation, and* RUTH *makes an effort. To* #1.) It's lovely country around here—
(They don't answer.)
(She struggles on to #4) It was lovely country all the way from New York—
(Same lack of reaction.)
In fact, it's all lovely, the whole country—from New York right to California. *(Crosses to Left, turns desperately)* I just love America!
(DAN *enters, carrying bag and hat box.*)

(RUTH *turns to him*) Where have you been the past three hours?

DAN. *(Putting the bags down)* Why? What's the matter?

RUTH. You'll find out. *(Cheerily turns to* MEN) Gentlemen, I'd like you to meet Dan King. *(Crosses to* #1, *at Right)* Dan, this is—er—er—Emile Schultz, I think—

AMISHMAN #1. Abner Zook.

RUTH. Of course— There are two of those. And this is—Franz Shubert?

AMISHMAN #2. Samuel Lapp.

RUTH. I'm sorry— And this is the other one, Abner Zook—

AMISHMAN #3. *(Hurt)* Ike Pilersheim.

RUTH. That's right. Sorry, Ike. *This* is the other Abner Zook.

AMISHMAN #4. Moses.

RUTH. *(Crossing to* DAN) Oh, yes! Abner Moses!

AMISHMAN #4. Moses Zook.

RUTH. I could have sworn there were two Abners. *(Crosses to* #5) And this gentleman is—er—Annheuser Busch?

AMISHMAN #5. Abner Zook.

RUTH. *(To* DAN) And you thought I was making it up! *(Up to the last one)* And Dan, *guess* who this is?—Jacob Yoder!

DAN. Oh?—Oh! How do you do—?

RUTH. Not Fat Jacob Yoder. Not Hairy Jacob Yoder. This is Jolly Jacob Yoder!

(JACOB *just stares.*)

DAN. I'm delighted to meet you, gentlemen. Why don't we all sit down?

RUTH. Dan, I've been through all that. They only stay a little.

DAN. Oh!— *(To the* AMISHMEN) It's lovely country around here—

RUTH. I'll save you a lot of time. *(To the* MEN) He loves America, too!

DAN. What?

RUTH. Come on, let's get unpacked—

(DAN *picks up the bags, and leads way around chair, toward door Right.*)

(RUTH *continues, from Right end of line)* Well, fellows— Keep the joint jumping!

(*As* RUTH *and* DAN *are about to leave,* EZRA *enters Right, carrying a large cabbage.*)

DAN. Oh! Hello—

(EZRA *stares at them, a little surprised.*)

I suppose you're another wedding guest.

EZRA. I am not a guest. I'm the one getting married.

DAN. Oh! Wonderful.

RUTH. Congratulations!

DAN. *(As* EZRA *continues staring)* Yes—er—that's certainly a fine-looking cabbage you have there.

EZRA. It's rotten!

DAN. Well—that's the way the world spins! Come on, Ruth—

(DAN *and* RUTH *exit Right.* ALL *look after them.* EZRA *shakes his head as he studies the cabbage.)*

JACOB. What are you so grumpy?

EZRA. *(Crossing and giving cabbage to* JACOB*)* My cabbages—all yellow by the edges.

JACOB. A man gets married Thursday should smile a little.

EZRA. Thursday I'll smile. Maybe.

SAMUEL LAPP. Ezra—you're glad to marry Katie, ain't?

EZRA. What's to be so glad?

SAMUEL LAPP. So why are you marrying Katie?

(SONG: "WHY NOT KATIE—EZRA AND THE MEN.)*

EZRA.

> Comes a time in his life
> When a man should take a wife;
> If I have to take a wife,
> So why not Katie?
>
> Milking cows Katie knows,
> Katie mends and Katie sews,
> And a farm with Katie goes,
> So why not Katie?
>
> It could be if I wait
> Comes along a perfect mate
> But for this a man could wait
> Until he's eighty.
>
> So in meeting when I stand
> With my hand in Katie's hand,
> And a wedding dinner making in the pot,
> When they ask, "Do you take Katie?"
> I will answer like a shot:
> "Do I take Katie—?
> Why not?"

SAMUEL LAPP.

> She's a nice girl, Katie always was.

EZRA.

> When her father says, 'Shut up' to her,
> She always does.

ABNER MOSES.
> You could marry Bertha Broder,
> Like a dream she cooks.

JACOB YODER.
> Like an ox she's healthy.

EZRA.
> Like an ox she looks!

ABNER ZOOK #1.
> Kate's a bissel skinny where she should be fat.

EZRA.
> When the kids start coming, she won't be so flat.

ABNER MOSES.
> With the hand of Anna Gruber comes a lot of cash.

EZRA.
> With the face of Anna Gruber comes a big moustache.

IKE PILERSHEIM.
> Once you promised Ilsa Brett
> When she grew up, you she'd get.

EZRA.
> But she ain't stopped growing yet,
> So I'll take Katie!

JACOB YODER.
> Once I kissed Dora Land!
> I found schmutzing Dora grand!

EZRA.
> So did half of Bird-in-Hand!
> So I'll kiss Katie.
>
> It could be if I wait,
> Comes along a perfect mate,

ALL.
> But for this a man could wait
> Until he's eighty.

EZRA.
> So tomorrow when I stand
> With my hand in Katie's hand
> And in meeting house they put me on the spot,
> In a clear and honest voice,
> Since I ain't got no other choice,
> I'll answer: "Katie—"

AMISHMEN.
> Sweet and lovely Katie—!

EZRA.
> Hard-working Katie!
> Why not?

(BLACKOUT. The portal plug flies in, and a bench is set down Left, in the dark.)

(LIGHTS come up on the next scene, as soon as set.)

ACT ONE

SCENE VI

Behind the Yoder house (in one).

Early evening.

As the LIGHTS come up, one romantic young AMISH COUPLE *is almost Center, crossing from Left to Right.* ANOTHER COUPLE *enters Left.* KATIE *comes in from Right, carrying copy-book, with the bluebird on the cover.*

1ST COUPLE. Hello, Katie.

(KATIE *acknowledges the greeting with a nod, and nods again to* 2ND COUPLE, *but she is preoccupied; crosses to the bench and sits.*)

DAN. *(After a moment, enters from Left)* Good evening, Katie—
KATIE. Oh. Hello. *(She closes the copy-book, and holds it on her lap.)*
DAN. I thought I'd take a look at my river farm. It's not far, is it?
KATIE. *(Rising)* No. If you want, I'll show you.
DAN. No hurry. That was a wonderful dinner, Katie.
KATIE. I'm glad you enjoyed.
DAN. That meat dish. I remember my grandmother used to make it. What do you call it again?
KATIE. Kassler Ripschen und Sauerkraut.
DAN. Your future husband is getting a great cook.
KATIE. Yah. *(Sits on bench, looks away)* That he knows.
DAN. Is anything the matter? Are you all right?
KATIE. I am all right. Sure.
DAN. You don't seem very happy—the day before your wedding.
KATIE. I am happy. Of course I am happy. Ezra is good Amish. Never does he make trouble. Why should I not be happy?
DAN. Of course. *(Sitting Left of her on bench)* How long have you two been engaged?
KATIE. It's maybe three months since Papa and Ezra's papa decided.
DAN. I see. That's the way it was arranged.
KATIE. Yah.
DAN. And you'll be living on the farm I'm selling your father.
KATIE. I guess.

DAN. *(Awkwardly)* Well—I hope you'll be very happy.

KATIE. Thank you.

DAN. *(Notices book)* What's that on the cover?

KATIE. This? A bluebird. It's my old school-book.

DAN. Curious looking thing. May I see it?

KATIE. Surely. *(She hands him the book.)*

DAN. Two eyes on one side of its head. *(Looks at her.)*

KATIE. *(Turning away)* Somebody made it for me once.

DAN. A boy?

KATIE. Yah—

DAN. *(Glances at her, leafs through book)* You weren't too good in arithmetic, Katie.

KATIE. No—

DAN. *(Still leafing through)* Say, this poem is charming. Did you write it?

KATIE. No, it's from around here. *(Hesitantly)* Somebody wrote it in for me.

DAN. Oh. The artist?

KATIE. *(Hesitates)* Yah—

DAN. *(Reads, as "YOUNG AND FOOLISH" is played under)*
"I love you so and we can get a house
    And you can fix it nice with paint—
    And when the stars is out, we'll feel so fine,
    But when the stars is all, you'll love me—ain't?"

KATIE. *(After a long pause, reminiscing, notices him watching her)* I'll show you the farm. *(She crosses quickly to Right, exits.)*

(DAN *follows to portal.*)

(The LIGHTS dim to out. In the dark, the house portal and plug fly out. When the LIGHTS come up again, the River Farm barn is revealed, with PETER *on stepladder, painting bluebird on barn.)*

ACT ONE

SCENE VII

A drop, in two, shows the barn on the River Farm. PETER, *on step-ladder, is pointing the finishing touches on a bluebird in a circle high on the barn wall. It resembles the one on* KATIE'S *copybook.*

(DAN *and* KATIE *appear down Right.* DAN *is carrying the copy-book. As they speak,* PETER *descends the ladder.)*

KATIE. *(Pointing out Right)* —And over that hill is the river.

DAN. Beautiful land. And all that is tobacco—!

KATIE. Corn!

DAN. I'd better brush up on my botany! But you do grow tobacco here?

KATIE. Yah. *(Turning, she crosses him)* Also grows here a lot of— *(She sees* PETER.*)*

PETER. Hello, Katie. *(Comes off ladder, sets paint can upstage.)*

KATIE. *(Crossing to Right Center)* Peter! You shouldn't have. —This is Mr. King. Peter Reber.

DAN. How do you do?

PETER. Hello.

DAN. That's an interesting bird you're painting there.

PETER. *(Looking at* KATIE*)* Yah.

DAN. *(Crossing* KATIE, *to Center)* These barn decorations are very colorful and— *(He looks at book cover, then at painting on barn, realizes significance. Hands book back to* KATIE*)* I'd better get back to the house— Ruth is waiting for me. Nice meeting you, Peter! *(He exits, down Left.)*

KATIE. You should not have done it, Peter!

PETER. *(Turning to her)* I'm going away, Katie. Tonight. I wanted you should remember me.

KATIE. *(Crosses in to Center)* You should not have done it.

PETER. *(Turns away)* If you want, I will paint it over.

KATIE. No—don't! Peter, you don't have to go away.

PETER. I want to.

KATIE. Please, Peter—! Please don't go away.

PETER. *(Turning slowly to face her)* Katie—Katie.

KATIE. *(Rushing into his arms)* Don't go away from me again, Peter!

PETER. I will talk to your father! He must listen to me!

KATIE. Not you, Peter. I will talk to him. To me he will listen.

PETER. You think, Katie?

KATIE. He must! I will make him listen! He must believe that you are good Amish. And you will be, ain't, Peter?

PETER. Yes, Katie.

KATIE. Not for Papa only. For me. Fighting is sinful. Promise me, Peter—never again—promise!

PETER. Never again. I promise!

(She has led him to down Right Center. They embrace.)

KATIE. Like it was a long time ago, ain't?

PETER. The best time it was—

*(REPRISE: "YOUNG AND FOOLISH"—*KATIE AND PETER.*)*

KATIE.
          Young and foolish,

It can't be wrong to be
Young and foolish—
We haven't long to be.
Soon enough the carefree days, the sunlit days go by,
Soon enough the bluebird has to fly.

PETER.

Call me foolish,
But I would choose to be,
Young and foolish,
The way we used to be

BOTH.

Smiling in the sunlight, laughing in the rain,
Together we'll be young and foolish again.

(At the start of the number, the LIGHTS begin to fade, until, by the end, the stage is completely dark, and PETER and KATIE are held only in the spotlights. They exit Right, and the SPOTS fade out.)

(In the darkness FOUR DANCERS enter from each side, carrying lanterns—BOYS from Right, GIRLS from Left. The lanterns give too little light for them to recognize each other, and in the darkness they call to one another.)

1ST BOY. Mary?
1ST GIRL. No, Deborah!
2ND BOY. Sarah?
2ND GIRL. No, Martha!
3RD BOY. Martha?
3RD GIRL. No, Sarah!

(They hang their lanterns on the stepladder, and the LIGHTS fade up again. They perform a romantic Lantern Dance, at the conclusion of which the BOYS take the GIRLS home, Right, and THREE of them cross lyrically to Left, suddenly realizing that they have left the FOURTH behind. ONE of them goes for him, and his GIRL, leaning from the portal, hands him his lantern, and a final kiss. The FOUR BOYS cross and exit Left.)

(During the dance, the bird-traveller has closed behind the DANCERS. It now opens on the little room under the stairs.)

ACT ONE

SCENE VIII

RUTH's *little room under the stairs. The door is in the Right wall, through a slanting ceiling, as if under stairs. There is a single bed with a patchwork quilt, an Amish chest at its foot. A dresser down Right with a lamp. There are hooks on the wall, either side of the up Center window, and a curtain strung on a shoulder-high pole across a jog in the set Left. There is no mirror or pictures.* RUTH'S *hatbox is on the bed, open.*

AT RISE: RUTH *is sprawled in a hard-back armchair, Left Center, smoking, and with a drink in her hand. A Scotch bottle is on the floor Left of the chest.*

RUTH. *(Toasting, bitterly)* To Hairy Jacob Yoder—! *(She drinks. She takes a puff, looks at the lengthening ash on the cigarette, finds no ash tray in evidence. She puts down her drink on the chest, considers and rejects her palm, crosses to the curtains and looks over them, rejecting that idea too. As she returns Center, she holds the top of her dress out for a moment, but gives that up. She sees the lamp on the dresser under the overhang, and starts for it, since it has a saucer base. But she bangs her head on the slanted ceiling, and grips it in mock agony)* This room was built for an Amish midget!
   (There is a KNOCK on the door.)
(She leaves the cigarette on the saucer base of the lamp) Who is it? *(Crossing to Left of the bed.)*
   DAN. *(Entering)* Hi— Just wanted to see if you were comfortable.
   RUTH. *(Getting dressing gown from hatbox)* Sure! I don't know why I let you drag me down here—
   DAN. *(After taking in slanting ceiling)* Now wait a minute— I didn't drag you. I asked you if you wanted to come, and you said yes.
   RUTH. *(Shakes out the robe)* Well, I thought you'd have been disappointed if I'd refused.
   DAN. I would have been. Very.
   RUTH. *(Warmly, crossing to Left of bed, and kneeling on it)* Would you, Dan?
   DAN. Of course— *(His eyes do not meet hers, but stray to the chest)* Say, I bet this chest is over two hundred years old!
   RUTH. *(Dryly, as she crosses and drapes robe over the curtain rod)* That's just what I was thinking!
   DAN. Well, I'm going to get unpacked. Anything you want?
   RUTH. *(Leaning on back of the armchair)* Nothing I can think of!
   DAN. See you later—

   (He exits—she looks after him—into song.)

(NUMBER: "HELLUVA WAY TO RUN A LOVE AFFAIR"—
Ruth.)

Ruth.
> In natural history every he,
> When wanting a particular she,
> Can always finds a way to tell her so.
> The cricket chirps, the penguin struts,
> The monkey tosses coconuts,
> The bullfrog makes a noise like Vaughn Monroe.
> What's true of bird and beast and bee
> Applies to people equally—
> Except for my particular Romeo.
>
> He may adore me—how would I know?
> If I'm the light of his life,
> It doesn't show.
> I go through the motions, but I'm well aware
> It's a helluva way to run a love affair!
>
> He doesn't tingle whenever we meet.
> Our love has all the thrill
> Of shredded wheat!
> We never run barefoot through each other's hair—
> It's a helluva way to run a love affair!
>
> Some lucky lovers have a talent for romance:
> Hackensack can seem like Paris, France.
> I have a true love with a different kind of knack:
> He turns Paris into Hackensack!
>
> I'm not suggesting he isn't A-1,
> He has a character like—George Washington!
> But when will my Georgie cross the Delaware?
> It's a helluva way to run a love affair!
>
> One enchanted evening, in my quiet living room,
> Candle-lit and heavy with perfume,
> Love songs I played him that sent shivers down his spine—
> And he fell in love with Oscar Hammerstein!
>
> For no good reason I'm hanging around;
> There must be some other fish that can be found!
> I'm stuck with the one I'm stuck on—c'est la guerre—
> My trustworthy, loyal, helpful, friendly—square!
> But it's a helluva way to run a love affair!

(Finishing the number, Ruth goes to the dresser for her cigarette.)
(There is a KNOCK on the door.)
Just a minute. Just a minute! *(She goes to the chest and drinks off*

*her unfinished Scotch and puts the glass under the pillow. She
recaps the bottle, and puts it in her hatbox.)*
   (Another KNOCK on the door.) .
In a second— Who is it? *(She starts for dresser, aware of the
cigarette, but remembers her previous bump and ducks. She gives
it up and crosses Left, cigarette behind her back)* Yes— Who is it?
(She is turning around, Left, as the door opens.)
   HILDA. *(Entering)* Excuse me—
      (RUTH straightens up, cigarette behind her back.)
You are ready for your bath?
   RUTH. I'd love it.
   HILDA. It will be ready soon now.
   RUTH. *(Coming in to Center)* Fine. By the way, Hilda, this
room doesn't seem to have a closet.
   HILDA. *(Coming in, Right Center)* No, we use the hooks.
(Sniffs) Something is brenning!
   RUTH. *(Also sniffing, to Left)* Brenning?
   HILDA. *(Right)* From a fire it smells.
   RUTH. *(Producing cigarette)* Oh, that's this.
   HILDA. *(Awed)* You were smoking it?
   RUTH. Well, yes— I was.
   HILDA. *(Sitting on the chest)* Uncle Jacob would have a connip-
tion!
   RUTH. I'm sorry—
   HILDA. *(Conspiratorial)* But what he don't know won't con-
niption him!
   RUTH. *(With sudden regard for the sisterhood)* Right! *(She is
still at a loss about what to do with the cigarette, and ad libs)*
Hilda, what shall I do—
   HILDA. *(Rises, extends hand)* I will throw it away. *(She takes
it to window, snuffs it out on the sill.)*
   RUTH. Hilda— Do Amish *men* smoke? *(She crosses to Right of
bed.)*
   HILDA. *(At window, up Center)* Some do. Young ones. But no
women—ever. She would be shunned.
   RUTH. *(Sitting on upstage end of the bed)* What do you mean?
   HILDA. *(Coming in)* Shunned. No one talks to you or looks at
you or anything. Shunned is a terrible thing. *(Picks up the stole
from foot of bed)* You want I should hang you up?
   RUTH. *(Double take, but realizes what HILDA means)* Thank
you, dear.
      *(HILDA hangs stole on upstage pegs. The door opens and the
      TWO YOUNG MILLERS enter with tub. They set it down, below
      RUTH, and stand staring at her.)*
Well, sir and madam— What is this?
   HILDA. For your bath. *(To the CHILDREN)* Get the hot water.
      (They stare at RUTH.)
Move once!

(The CHILDREN *scurry out of the room.)*

RUTH. Hilda— No indoor plumbing?

HILDA. *(Crosses up Right Center slightly)* By us plain Amish, such a thing is not allowed.

RUTH. *(Incredulous)* Nobody has plumbing!?

HILDA. *(With stole)* Well—a few fancy ones.

RUTH. I see. The button crowd! *(She gets slippers from hatbox)* Well, bath time! *(She pulls tub behind curtains, draws them, and starts undressing.)*

HILDA. I'll finish putting away for you. *(Picks up dress)* Golly, what soft goods! *(She puts it down beside hat-box, and picks up a pair of panties)* What is this?

RUTH. *(Looks over pole, busy with her undressing)* Panties.

(HILDA *is baffled.)*

You know—underwear.

HILDA. Oh—these go under the bloomers.

RUTH. Bloomers? I don't wear bloomers.

HILDA. *(Astounded)* Just these?

RUTH. That's all.

HILDA. *(Crossing for* RUTH's *shoes)* This would give Mama a conniption!—The shoes I'll put under the bed here. *(She crosses back to bed, puts shoes away, panties on top of skirt.)*

RUTH. Fine.

HILDA. *(After a moment)* You are keeping company with Mr. King—steady-like?

RUTH. Dan? Hmmm—no. Not what you'd call steady-like.

HILDA. *(Crossing to get* RUTH's *slip from pole)* He is a very interesting-looking man.

RUTH. Yes, he is.

HILDA. He's wonderful nice.

RUTH. Mm. I hope this tub doesn't give me any splinters anywhere.

HILDA. *(Hangs slip stage Left jog, then comes down and leans over chair back)* I looked at Mr. King's fingers already. They are very clean.

RUTH. Yes—

HILDA. Like a dentist! *(She picks up brassiere from pole)* Very polite he is also, and— *(Notices bra)* —What is *this* thing?

RUTH. *(Looking over the curtain)* What do you think it is?

HILDA. *(Holding it by the shoulder straps, so that it looks like a basket)* For carrying things?

RUTH. No, dear, it—well, *yes,* in a way! Look it's for— *(Indicates on herself with a little clumsy embarrassment)* You wear it. Around here.

HILDA. It's wonderful fancy! *(She hangs it next to the slip, crosses to the bed, gets the Scotch bottle out of the hat-box, and looks at it)* You want I should put this away for you?

RUTH. That? No, dear, I'll put that away myself.

HILDA. *(Replaces Scotch bottle, and holds up a red dress)* Look at this once!

RUTH. You like it? It's yours!

HILDA. Me? How could I wear this ever?

(She starts to hang up the dress, up Center, when the TWO CHILDREN *enter.)*

(She addresses them) So where is the water?

BOY. Papa wants the tub once. *(He starts behind the upstage edge of the curtain as* HILDA *hangs up the dress.)*

RUTH. *(Yelps)* Wait a minute once!

(The BOY *retreats.* RUTH *hastily puts on robe, and comes out at downstage edge of curtain.)*

HILDA. Where are you going to take the tub?

BOY. The sick calf— Papa wants to wash him down.

(The GIRL *goes behind curtains for tub.)*

RUTH. *(Coming from behind curtain)* But what about my bath?

BOY. *(Going down to her)* You can take a bath after the calf.

(He goes into alcove for one end of the tub, and with the GIRL *carrying the other end, starts for the door.)*

RUTH. Forget it! Don't bring it back—ever!

(The CHILDREN *exit with tub.)*

HILDA. By the kitchen sink you can wash a little.

RUTH. That'll have to do. *(She crosses to Right Center.)*

HILDA. *(After a moment)* It wonders me something.

RUTH. What is it now—the girdle?

HILDA. It wonders me that a person like you, with such a pretty face, is not yet married.

RUTH. Well, I was married. *(She closes the hatbox.)*

HILDA. Oh. He died by you, the husband?

RUTH. No, but it's a lovely idea. We were divorced.

HILDA. *(Amazed)* Divorced yet!

RUTH. Hilda, where is the—er—ladies room—the—er—

HILDA. *(Simply)* The toilet?

RUTH. You do talk loud and clear, don't you? Where is it?

HILDA. Outside, in the back.

RUTH. I should have known. *(She crosses down for the hand towel on the downstage end of the dresser.)*

(DAN enters.)

Hello, Clean Fingers!

DAN. *(Looks at his hand, confused)* Where are you going?

RUTH. Outside—in the back— Stay a little yet, already, any-how—once.

(RUTH *exits, and* DAN *starts to follow.*)

HILDA. Mr. King—

DAN. *(Turns to her)* Yes, Hilda?

HILDA. Er— You want I should help in your room?

DAN. No, thanks. Everything's all right. *(He starts to go again, but pauses in the doorway, thoughtfully)* Oh, Hilda.

HILDA. *(Smoothing the coverlet, flustered)* Yah, Mr. King?

DAN. *(Hesitantly)* Who is this fellow Peter?

HILDA. *(Puts hat-box on floor, above bed)* Peter? He is Ezra's brother.

DAN. I know, but I was wondering—about him and Katie.

HILDA. Oh. That. *(Busy with the bed)* They were ferliebt since they were kids yet.

DAN. Oh?

HILDA. But Katie's papa never liked him, and— *(She finds glass under the pillow)* Look—under the pillow!

(She starts to sniff, but DAN *quickly takes it from her and sniffs himself.)*

DAN. *(Crossing to dresser, puts glass down)* Yes! Ruth's been taking her vitamins. I hope your father lets you marry a man you choose.

HILDA. I hope. *(She crosses to rod, gets* RUTH'S *dress)* It would be pleasant when you marry a man you would also like him.

DAN. *(Amused, sits on the chest)* That's true. And you have a pretty way of putting things.

HILDA. Pretty? Me?

DAN. I meant— Well, yes. You are a pretty girl.

HILDA. *(At Left of armchair)* I guess where you come from all girls are pretty-like.

DAN. Where in the world did you get that idea?

HILDA. Sometimes they pass by here in their cars, and they're always so shiny.

DAN. The cars.

HILDA. The people too—you know? Sometimes I think of how it is outside of here.

DAN. And how do you think it is?

HILDA. Well—everything is polished like silver—and the people walk light—and there's a lot of laughing.

DAN. Don't you like it here, Hilda?

HILDA. Oh, yah. I like it fine. It is a happy life here.

DAN. But you think about other places?

HILDA. Sometimes. *(She sits on Left arm of chair)* I would like to see how it is maybe—once. Sometimes I see an airplane, and I think what kind of man is up there, flying through the clouds? I guess a lean man, and tall—and without a beard.

DAN. I see—

HILDA. I think it is all like that. The girls are pretty and the men are tall and they move through the sky.

DAN. It isn't quite like that, Hilda. The men are not all tall, and the girls certainly aren't all as pretty as you are.

HILDA. You think?

DAN. I know. Not as pretty or as charming. The fellow who gets you will be very lucky.

HILDA. *(Flustered, she goes up, hangs the dress on the Left jog)* Also I cook good.

DAN. I know you do.

HILDA. *(Turning to DAN)* Also children I like.

DAN. *(Rises, crosses up Right of bed)* Hilda, how old are you?

HILDA. I'm twenty-two.

DAN. Twenty-two. That's a wonderful age.

HILDA. You think? *(Crossing to chest, she kneels on it)* Papa worries I'm getting to be an old one.

DAN. Old? Why, you're young—and sweet and radiant.

HILDA. What does that mean?

DAN. Why—full of life; refreshing—

HILDA. *(Rising on her knees)* Refreshing?

DAN. Well, that means—

HILDA. I think it means you like me, ain't? *(By now her face is close to his.)*

DAN. Of course I do. You're—I guess the right word is—enchanting.

HILDA. What does that mean?

DAN. It means— *(He takes her face in his hand and kisses her lightly. He goes to the door, turns back and smiles at her, then exits.)*

(HILDA *is transfixed.*)

(SONG: "THIS IS ALL VERY NEW TO ME"—HILDA.)

HILDA.
> All at once the room is reeling,
> Bells are pealing,
> Butterflies are fluttering inside.
> *(She rises slowly, and moves down into One.)*
> All at once I get to feeling
> Just like a new-born bride.

(The bird-traveller closes behind her. During the next chorus, she is joined from Left by a TRIO OF GIRLS.*)*

> This is all very new to me,
> This is all very fine,
> This so sunny-like,
> Sort of funny-like,
> Milk-and-honey-like feeling of mine.
> This is all very new to me
> And I'm knocking on wood.
> What to do? What to say?
> How to make it go on this way?
> Wish that I understood,

TRIO.

> Do you seem to float in space?

HILDA.

> With the silliest look on my face
> And a light in my eye.

TRIO.

> Do you feel all out of breath?

HILDA.

> Upside down, scared to death!

TRIO.

> Are you wondering why?

HILDA.

> It's as simple as pie!

(The traveller opens behind them on the Yoder yard.)

ACT ONE

SCENE IX

The Yoder yard.

AMISH YOUNG PEOPLE *are playing in the yard, tossing bean bags, balls, etc. As the traveller opens, they quiet down, and* HILDA *sings the second chorus to various groups of them.*

HILDA.

> This is all very new to me,
> Has me all in a haze.

GIRLS.

> Now you know about
> What they glow about—

HILDA.

> And I go about shouting its praise!

> This is all very new to me,
> And I'm knocking on wood.
> What to do? What to say?
> How to make it go on this way?
> Wish that I understood,
> 'Cause it feels oh so good!
> So wonderful good!

(A dance follows, involving HILDA *and the* YOUNG PEOPLE. *It is twice interrupted by groups of* WEDDING GUESTS *arriving with gifts, and dressed in black capes and bonnets, and disapproving of the fun. The dance ends with* HILDA *down Left, and she sings:)*

HILDA.

> What to do? What to say?
> How to make it go on this way?
> Wish that I understood,
> 'Cause it feels oh so good!
> So wonderful good!

(During the breakup, EZRA *crosses from Left, in Two, carrying folding chairs.* TWO BOYS *roll the wagon back down in place, and check the wheels.)*

AMISHMAN. *(Coming from Right in One with his wife)* See? There's still more buggies coming. I told you we're not late!

AMISH WOMAN. *(To* ANOTHER WOMAN, *crossing from down Left and going into the house)* You heard? Amos Lapp and all are coming for the wedding Thursday—all the way from Lebanon!

*(*PAPA *enters down Left, followed by* DAN.*)*

PAPA. *(Stopping below the wagon)* —So tell me your price. I am ready to pay cash.

DAN. Mr. Yoder, you don't have to pay the whole thing in cash. I don't mind taking a mortgage for part of it.

PAPA. *(Moving Center)* We don't like mortgages. If we ain't got cash, we don't buy.

SAMUEL. *(Entering from up Left and crossing down)* Jacob, hello!

(They shake hands.)

This time next year you'll be a grandfather!

PAPA. I hope. Go inside. Everybody's by the parlor.

*(*SAMUEL *goes into house.)*

DAN. You're having quite a few visitors tonight.

PAPA. Before a wedding, people visit, to enjoy a little. *(Pause)* Yah. On the River Farm, they will have a happy life, Katie and Ezra.

DAN. I hope so—

PAPA. Twenty-five acres, and a good big house. I always wanted to do the best for Katie.

DAN. Well— Mr. Yoder, I don't think Katie's marrying the man she really wants.

PAPA. *(Turning to him)* What are you talking? Who does she want?

DAN. She's in love with Peter, Mr. Yoder.

PAPA. That one! A trouble maker. He was sent away from here for making trouble, for fighting. In love—she wants—! *(He crosses angrily away from DAN to Right Center.)*

AMISHMAN. *(Coming from up Left, crossing around PAPA)* Jacob, my cousin Aaron is here yet?

PAPA. *(Crossly)* I guess. Or else not.

(The AMISHMAN does a take, and goes into house.)

DAN. Just talk to her for a minute, Mr. Yoder. Why, when I saw Peter painting that bird on the barn, I was sure—

PAPA. He painted a bird?

DAN. On the barn, on my property. Mr. Yoder, Katie and Peter grew up together, they—

PAPA. What kind of a bird?

DAN. *(Realizing he has said the wrong thing, moves a little down Left)* Oh, I don't know. A thing with both eyes on one side of its head. Look, I know all this is none of my business, but—

PAPA. That's a funny thing to paint where Ezra and Katie will live—

(KATIE enters from down Left and crosses to Center, between PAPA and DAN.)

KATIE. Papa. Can I talk to you once?

PAPA. You saw Peter!

KATIE. *(After an accusing look at DAN)* Yes, I did!

PAPA. I told you not to!

KATIE. But anyway I saw him. That is why I want to talk with you.

PAPA. There is nothing to talk! Go into the house with the company.

(Several AMISH enter.)

AMISH WOMAN. Katie, wait till you see my wedding present! Come inside.

KATIE. I will talk with you, Papa. If not now, later! *(She gives* DAN *another look and goes into house with the* AMISH WOMAN.)

PAPA. That one had to come back!

DAN. Mr. Yoder, how can you force a girl to marry a man you've picked out for her?

(AMISHMEN *start entering.)*

PAPA. *(To* DAN) We do not force! A father knows only that he is smarter than a child yet.

DAN. *(Crossing away to down Left)* But there's such a thing as being too strict.

PAPA. *(Going to* DAN) Strict is our way of living, Mister. Strict is how we live, and plain, and simple—and content.

DAN. But, look Mr. Yoder, times have changed. You just can't—

(SONG: "PLAIN WE LIVE"—PAPA AND AMISHMEN.)

PAPA.

> Let me say it once, Mister,
> We know how we want it here.
> We know who we are, Mister.
> Don't interfere.
> We don't need a city man, with city soft words,
> To tell us what to do.
> Go upon your way, Mister,

CHORUS *and* PAPA.

> We got our own way too.

PAPA.

> Plain we live,
> For plain we see,
> It's good for people to live plain.

CHORUS *and* PAPA.

> Hard we work so life is good.
> When life is hard we don't complain.

PAPA.

> Strangers look on us and call us strange,
> But cheat we don't, and steal we don't,
> And wars we don't arrange.

CHORUS *and* PAPA.

> Plain we live,
> For plain is good,
> And plain is how we mean to stay.
> To God we pray to keep us plain.

(The MUSIC continues under the following dialogue.)

PAPA. Look around you, Mister! Look in your world, and look

here! Poor people you have plenty, and worried people, and afraid. Here we are not afraid. We do not have all your books, and your learning, but we know what is right. We do not destroy, we build only.

CHORUS *and* PAPA.

> Strangers look on us and call us strange,
> But cheat we don't, and steal we don't,
> And wars we don't arrange.

*(*PAPA *crosses to Right Center, and the* MEN *move down for the ending.)*

> Plain we live,
> For plain is good,
> And plain is how we mean to stay.
> To God we pray to keep us plain.

(They exit at end of song, leaving DAN *alone. He lights a cigarette, and crosses up, half-sits on wagon, between front and rear wheels.* PETER *enters from Right, in agitation.)*

PETER. Mr. King—

DAN. What is it, Peter?

PETER. Mr. King, I want to buy your River Farm.

DAN. You want to buy it?

PETER. Tell me how much, Mr. King! Almost three hundred dollars I have saved up. The rest I could pay off from the crops.

DAN. Peter, I told Mr. Yoder I'd sell it to him. That's why I came down here.

PETER. I hoped always some day to live on that farm—with Katie!

DAN. Peter, having the farm won't help you. Mr. Yoder wouldn't call off the marriage, even if I didn't sell it to him.

PETER. I do not know. But I must try. Tell me only how much!

*(*EZRA *enters from the house. There is a flash of LIGHTNING and a clap of THUNDER.)*

EZRA. *(Crosses to Right of* PETER, *observing the storm warnings, speaks good-naturedly)* Peter! Give me a help once, will you? In the buggy there, I brought extra chairs for the company.

PETER. *(Crossing away to down Left, below wagon)* I am busy, Ezra. I am talking.

EZRA. *(To* DAN*)* Did you finish with Mr. Yoder about the farm, yet?

DAN. Not yet. *(He rises, and crosses slowly away to Right, listening but not watching.)*

EZRA. *(To* PETER, *who has his back turned)* I'll have a job for you on the farm, if you want, Peter—

PETER. I don't want!

EZRA. *(Crosses down to* PETER, *below wagon)* You still fer-hoodled about Katie? *(To* DAN, *as* PETER *does not answer)* He is still ferhoodled about Katie!

(Clap of THUNDER and flash of LIGHTNING.)

*(*EZRA *glances up at approaching storm)* It's going to come down soon rain.

(To PETER, *who turns upstage.)*

Don't stand like a lummox. Help out a little with the chairs. It's for the wedding, Peter. Katie's wedding. You always wanted to be by Katie's wedding, ain't?—So you'll be, but in the back! I'll be in the front! Don't be so ferhoodled about Katie. She's a girl, like all girls. There are plenty of girls left for you.

(He laughs. PETER *crosses upstage Center,* EZRA *following.)*

Come on, pick up a chair. Maybe I'll let you kiss the bride! You'll enjoy to kiss Katie, ain't? I'll let you kiss her, but no pinch-ing!

*(*DAN, *realizing* EZRA's *needling, drops cigarette and stamps on it.* PETER, *in a rage, attacks* EZRA, *who falls backward to the ground,* PETER *on top of him, pummelling him. They roll over twice, and* DAN *pulls* PETER *off of* EZRA.)*

DAN. Peter, stop it! Let him go! This won't get you anywhere!

*(*EMMA, HILDA, PAPA, KATIE, SAMUEL *and* AMISHMEN *and* WOMEN *run out of the house.* SAMUEL *goes quickly to* PETER, *locks his arms around him, taking over from* DAN.)*

AMISHMAN #1. It's Peter. He's fighting again!

EMMA. *(On porch with* HILDA) Stop him, somebody!

SAMUEL. *(Struggling with* PETER) Peter, stop! You can't fight your own brother!

KATIE. *(Getting hold of* PETER, *down Center)* Peter, you promised—you promised!

EZRA. *(Dragged off to Left Center)* He is crazy, that one!

PAPA. *(At Right Center)* He is a man of violence!

AMISHMAN #2. *(At down Left Center, looking off Left)* What is that over there?

EZRA. Where?

AMISHMAN #2. Look! Smoke!

AMISHMAN #1. *(At extreme down Right)* Something is bren-ning!

SAMUEL. Looks like a haystack—

PAPA. No! It's too big a fire for that!

EZRA. It's the barn! On your farm! *(He runs off Left.)*

*(*HILDA *and* EMMA *run to Right of the wagon.)*

AMISHMAN #3. *(Running on from up Left and exiting down Right)* Jacob! We need buckets!

DAN. What can I do to help?

PAPA. *(Pointing off down Right)* Quick! Get buckets in my barn!

(DAN rushes off Right, where he sheds his jacket and tie.)

AMISHMAN #4. *(From Left in Two, exiting down Right)* Also, we'll need axes!

SAMUEL. *(Going off Left, in One)* Get the animals out first!

PAPA. *(At Center, directing)* Run over to the Rebers' and get help!

EMMA. *(Running off Right in Two, as HILDA runs off Left, above wagon)* Hilda! Find the children!

(As PAPA moves down to One, the landscape-traveller closes above him, Right to Left.)

AMISHMAN #3. *(To One, Right to Left)* Where shall we bring everything?

PAPA. Get the buckets. Save what you can! Bring everything into my barn! *(He exits Left.)*

AMISHMAN #5. *(From Right with axe)* Bring it in the Yoder barn!

SAMUEL. *(From Left with sack)* Get more buckets!

AMISHMAN #6. *(From Left with harness and sack)* The smoke —you can't get in there no more!

AMISHMAN #2. *(From Right to Left, with bucket)* We'll try to save something at least!

(Through the landscape-traveller is seen a silhouette against a plain red sky; PEOPLE rushing across, carrying farm implements, OTHERS on wagon, beckoning, etc.)

JACOB. *(The last one to cross Left to Right)* Help! Help!

(The silhouette fades, and the scene returns to One, in front of the traveller.)

DAN. *(Enters from Right with two buckets)* Did they get the animals out?

AMISHMAN #5. *(Crossing from Left with bucket)* I think!

HILDA. *(Entering from Left with the TWO CHILDREN)* It's no use—it's no use— *(She stops DAN at down Left, after crossing him)* Don't go! Nobody can go near it no more—it's brenning terrible fast!

DAN. *(Looking off)* It went up like a matchbox!

HILDA. Yah—it started so sudden! How could it happen?
DAN. It must have been struck by lightning!
HILDA. I guess!
    (AMISHMAN #2 *comes from Left with sack.*)
Bring it in the Yoder barn. Everything we're bringing there!
    DAN. Better get the kids into the house! I'll see if they need help in the Yoder barn. (DAN *exits Left.*)

(HILDA *goes off Right with the* CHILDREN.)

ACT ONE

SCENE X

(The landscape-traveller opens on the Yoder barn. Some of the AMISH *are already there.)*

    PAPA. *(Running in from Left, following* SEVERAL MEN) Is everybody all right? Did anybody get hurt?
    SAMUEL. *(Following him)* No! I never saw anything go up so fast!
    EZRA. *(From Left to Left of Center with two buckets)* Mr. Yoder! The barn is all!
    PAPA. *(Right of Center)* I know. I know also what made it!

(He glares at PETER, *who has come from Left, and meets* KATIE, *coming from Right.* DAN *enters from Left, crosses to Center.* HILDA *comes down to his Left.)*

    DAN. Probably struck by lightning!
    PAPA. It was a hex!
    ALL. A hex—
    PAPA. His hex!
    DAN. But, Mr. Yoder. That's ridiculous!
    PAPA. He is our trouble. We will manage it. We! Not you.
    RACHEL. *(Far Right)* I seen the hex! It was a bluebird thing!
    PETER. That was not a hex!
    KATIE. *(Crosses* PETER *to* PAPA) That was not a hex, Papa!
    PAPA. *(Pushing her upstage, so he can face* PETER, *who is Right Center)* It was. You done it. You wanted her! Even your own brother you struck!
    DAN. Now wait, Mr. Yoder!
    PAPA. *(To* PETER, *ignoring* DAN) This is not the first time you have made trouble here. You are not a plain man. You have violence in you. For this you will be punished! For this you will be shunned!
    HILDA. *(As* DAN *looks at her questioningly)* Shunned. Is a terrible thing!

(The ENSEMBLE *on stage are frozen for a moment, staring at*
PETER. DAN *starts to approach him, as if to help, but* HILDA
*stops him and leads him off Left. The "Plain We Live" theme
starts quietly, and* AMISHMEN *and* WOMEN *slowly start exiting, turning away from* PETER *as they pass him. The* ENSEM-
BLE *start singing "Plain We Live," the* DANCERS *slowly exiting, as they shun* PETER. PETER *goes to* EZRA, *appealing to
him, but* EZRA *turns from him, picks up his buckets and goes
out Left. Same business with* SAMUEL. PETER *looks towards*
KATIE, *who is with* PAPA *down Right. She rushes to him, want-
ing to embrace him. But as she reaches him, she turns toward
her father, remembers her duty as an Amish girl, and exits
down Right.* PAPA *and* RACHEL *follow her off.* PETER *is left in
stage Center, in a SPOT, with the* MALE CHORUS *at the Left,
singing "Plain We Live.")*

(The SCRIM LIGHTS up and behind the barn we see AMISHMEN
and WOMEN *solemnly walking from Right to Left and up
ramp and off.* KATIE *is the last one. At the top of the ramp
she turns for a moment to look at* PETER. *Their eyes meet, but
she shuns him and walks off. With the last note of the song,
the* CHORUS *exits Right and Left, leaving* PETER *alone on
stage, deserted and shunned.)*

("PLAIN WE LIVE"—REPRISE—ACT ONE FINALE.)

CHORUS.

> Plain we live
> For plain we see
> It's good for people to live plain.
>
> Hard we work
> So life is good;
> When life is hard we don't complain.
>
> To our Amish way we must be true,
> For here we stay to keep the faith,
> The faith our fathers knew.
>
> Plain we live,
> For plain is good,
> And plain is how we mean to stay!
> To God we pray
> To keep us plain!

(The House Curtain comes in slowly.)

END OF ACT ONE

ACT TWO

SCENE I

Site of the burned barn on the River Farm.

The stone foundation of the barn is up Center, and the stone spring house adjacent to it, Left, is intact. There are a few sticks of charred wood still standing.

The Amish community, men and women alike, are working with saws hammers, planes, etc., on pieces of the new barn, which is about to be erected. The group includes PAPA, EZRA, ISAAC, HILDA, SAMUEL and JACOB.

At the end of the entr-acte music, the busy, gay scene is revealed through the map scrim, which flies out on the 7th bar of the intro to the number.

(SONG: "HOW DO YOU RAISE A BARN"—PAPA, EZRA, HILDA AND COMPANY.)

ALL.
>How do you raise a barn?
>How do you raise a barn?
>You raise a barn with nails and wood,
>With nails and wood and schwitzing good,
>It comes a barn!

(DAN *enters from Left. Activity with the components of the new barn resumes.*)

DAN. *(To PAPA, Left of Center)* Hello, Mr. Yoder. Where did all these people come from?
PAPA. When we have a barn raising, people come from all over to help.
DAN. You mean they all volunteer to work like this?
HILDA. *(Left of DAN)* By us a barn raising means to help and enjoy!
DAN. You'll be at this for weeks—
PAPA. Not us, Mr. King! Just wait and see!

51

ALL.
> How do you raise a barn?
> How do you raise a barn?
> You raise a barn with careful hands,
> So strong it looks and strong it stands!
> With careful hands, so strong it stands!
> With nails and wood, and schwitzing good!
> It comes a barn!

(As the MUSIC continues under, ladders are brought on from Right and Left, and the framework of the new barn is erected. When nearly completed, the CHORUS resumes:)

ALL.
> How do you raise a barn?
> How do you raise a barn?
> You raise it with your neighbor,
> Who helps you with your labor—
> Who works all day with careful hands,
> With careful hands, so strong it stands,
> With nails and wood and schwitzing good!
> It comes a barn! A barn! A barn!

(The MUSIC continues under, as before, while the face pieces of the barn are fastened in place, like a jig-saw puzzle. Just as the roof is finally hooked in place, the CHORUS sings:)

ALL.
> That's how you raise a barn!
> With nails and wood, and schwitzing good,
> It comes a barn!

(On the last note, the weather-vane appears in place, and triumphant faces lean from various doors in the completed building.
> *During the play-out music, the ladders are removed; the saw-horse table is moved two feet to Center by two BOYS; and the nail keg is placed Left of it.*
> *The CROWD disperses. DAN gets some nut strudel from RACHEL, who has come in earlier with a basket of refreshments for the workers. He then goes up. PAPA and EZRA are down Left Center.*
> *HILDA exits down Right.)*

AMISHMAN #1. *(To EZRA)* It'll be a better barn than it was before.

EZRA. Yah! *(To PAPA)* Looks real solid, ain't?

PAPA. The old barn was solid also.

AMISHMAN #2. *(To* EZRA*)* A terrible thing to happen, just before your wedding.

ISAAC. Funny, Peter was always—

PAPA. I want no talk of Peter! Let him stay shunned!

*(*PAPA *and* EZRA *exit up Left, returning with screwdrivers, with which they work on the barn door.* ISAAC *is busy with a zig-zag rule.* DAN *is with them, trying to help.* HILDA *enters from Right, in Two, with a pitcher and glasses on a tray. She puts them down on the saw-horse table, and starts to pour.)*

JACOB. *(Crossing to table Right of* HILDA*)* Hilda! You got something to drink? I'm busting from the heat!

HILDA. Here— *(She hands* JACOB *a drink.)*

JACOB. *(Taking it)* Hilda—you want maybe to go with me later, over by the lake?

HILDA. No.

JACOB. *(As* AMISHMAN #1, *who has been touching up the barn with paint, comes down for a drink)* It will be cool, sitzing by the lake.

HILDA. So go sitz! *(Gives* AMISHMAN #1 *a glass.)*

(He drinks it and exits Right, leaving glass on ground, Right of the ramp.)

JACOB. Why don't you want to come with me?

HILDA. *(As* AMISHMAN #3 *comes down for drink)* Because I don't want to.

JACOB. Because why not?

HILDA. *(Giving* AMISHMAN #3 *his glass)* Because you're skinny!

*(*AMISHMAN #3 *resumes his painting.)*

JACOB. What's skinny got to do?

HILDA. Finish with your drink once!

*(*AMISHMAN #4 *comes down.)*

JACOB. Because I'm skinny just, you won't go? *(He scratches himself vigorously.)*

HILDA. *(Giving glass to* AMISHMAN #4, *who goes upstage)* Also, you're all the time crotzing!

JACOB. *(Stops scratching abruptly)* What's crotzing got to do?

*(*AMISHMAN #2 *crosses down.)*

HILDA. Give me the glass once!

JACOB. Hilda, come with me by the lake.

HILDA. Leave me be. Find a girl who enjoys a skinny crotzer! *(Gives glass to* AMISHMAN #2.)

(AMISHMAN #4 *has returned with an empty one.)*

AMISHMAN #2. It's no use, Jacob. This one likes *no* feller!

HILDA. Maybe.

AMISHMAN #4. Maybe? You found a feller, Hilda? *(He hands her his glass.)*

HILDA. Maybe.   . .

AMISHMAN #2. Look how she looks! Not maybe! For sure!

JACOB. *(Gesturing to illustrate his lines, as* HILDA *refills* AMISHMAN'S #4 *glass)* So who is it once? Not fat. Not skinny. Not big. Not little. Not a crotzer. Not ferhoodled—

HILDA. Also, not fershpritzed! *(She throws the water from the glass in his face and runs off Right, laughing.)*

(RUTH, *coming in from Right 1½, almost runs into her.)*

RUTH. *(Looking after* HILDA) Well, that's a happy one.

AMISHMAN #2. *(At Left of saw-horse table)* Sure! She found a feller!

RUTH. Really? Who's the lucky boy?

JACOB. *(Drying himself)* Not any fellow from around here, for sure!

AMISHMAN #4. Not one of us, for sure.

(He returns to his painting with AMISHMAN #2. JACOB *exits, Right, in Two.* DAN *has backed downstage, Left Center, admiring the completed barn.)*

RUTH. *(Glancing at* DAN, *then after the departed* HILDA) He always did like buttermilk!

(AMISHMEN #2 *and* #4 *drift off Right.)*

DAN. *(Seeing* RUTH) Ruth, you should have seen these people pitch in and work together—and did you taste this nut strudel? It's sensational! These people know how to live!

RUTH. *(Crosses to keg, Center, and sits on it)* Dan, why don't you buy a big black hat and move in?

DAN. Hilda made it.

RUTH. Oh?

DAN. That kid's a great cook!

RUTH. *(Testing him)* Cute, too!

DAN. She sure is! And you know, she's very bright—

RUTH. I know. We had a long talk about underwear.

DAN. *(Crosses to above saw-horse table)* And she's so honest!
No pretenses. Just—just—

RUTH. Just plain folks? She's quite young, though, isn't she?

DAN. No. She's twenty-two. She just has a very youthful quality.

RUTH. At twenty-two, what's the trick?

DAN. Who'd ever expect to find a girl like Hilda in this kind of
place?

    (PAPA finishes with doors, starts to cross downstage Center.)
I thought they'd all be much more—

PETER. *(Enters from down Left, crosses to PAPA)* Mr. Yoder—

    (DAN stops. EZRA and ISAAC stop working.)

PAPA. *(Calling Right)* David, you can start putting the hay in
the barn now.

PETER. Mr. Yoder, it was not a hex on the barn!

(PAPA crosses back to up Left Center, ignoring PETER, as do the
OTHERS.)

EZRA. *(To PAPA)* It is a nervy thing how a man who is shunned
tries to talk to others.

AMISHMAN #2. It wouldn't wonder me if he had nerve even to
come to your wedding.

EZRA. After fighting and hexing my farm, even!

PETER. *(To EZRA)* It is not yet your farm.

EZRA. *(To AMISHMEN)* Enough for now, ain't? Time to eat!
(He stalks off Right, in One.)

(The OTHERS follow up Right. RUTH rises, and crosses to Right of
table, awed and worried. PETER, alone and defeated, starts
off Left.)

DAN. Peter!

    (PETER continues to leave, and DAN crosses down to him.)
Peter!

    (PETER turns as DAN gets to him. RUTH watches.)
Peter, I'm sorry. I feel somehow that I caused all this.

PETER. No, it was not you. I am leaving here.

DAN. Where are you going?

PETER. Some place. I do not know for sure yet.

DAN. If there's anything at all I can do—

PETER. Maybe the farm—if I had that— *(He shakes his head*
and breaks off, then crosses DAN to Center) No, you were right. It
would not help.

(KATIE enters from down Right with a basket to collect the pitcher
and glasses. RUTH gives up, slightly, watching. KATIE does not

see PETER *until they meet at Center. They look at each other for a moment, then she speaks to* DAN.)

KATIE. Lunch is ready, Mr. King! *(She crosses up to get glass on ground by ramp.)*
DAN. Peter is leaving, Katie.

(She doesn't answer.)

PETER. *(Crosses up to* KATIE, *kneeling beside her)* Katie, come with me.
KATIE. *(Her determination wins out and she crosses to above the table with the basket)* I must not talk to him, Mr. King. He is shunned. *(She attempts to collect the rest of the glasses.)*
DAN. *(At up Left Center)* But, Katie—
KATIE. *(Sharply, very hurt)* I am yet Amish, Mr. King! He is shunned!

(RUTH *attempts a gesture, but* DAN *motions to her as he crosses, and they* BOTH *leave down Right.* KATIE *attempts to leave also, but* PETER *crosses to Right, intercepting her.)*

PETER. Katie, you want to come with me—you know you do!
    (She goes around Left end of table, but again he stops her, going around Right end of table.)
Katie, listen—listen once—if not to me—to your own self.

*(SONG: "FOLLOW YOUR HEART"—*PETER.)

PETER.

Follow your heart
Whenever it calls to you,
Whatever it tells you to do.
The heart has reasons
The mind cannot know.
Follow your heart
Wherever it wants you to go.

Lost in the night
You wonder what path to take
'Til a whisper comes through:
Come out of the darkness
Into the day!
Your heart knows the way!
Follow your heart.

To the someone who needs you,
As he did from the start;
To the someone who waits for you
To follow your heart.

(He has seated her on the nail keg and is kneeling Right of her. She breaks away, and runs down Left.)

PETER. Katie—

(But she won't stop. Down Left, she meets HILDA, who has entered from Left Two, and heard the last few lines of the song.)

(The landscape-traveller closes from the Right, hiding PETER but leaving KATIE and HILDA in One.)

KATIE. I must not listen to him, ain't? I am doing right, ain't, Hilda?

HILDA. I do not know for sure. I feel only one thing—

(REPRISE: "FOLLOW YOUR HEART"—HILDA AND KATIE.)

HILDA.

> Follow your heart
> Whenever it calls to you,
> Whatever it tells you to do.
> The heart has reasons
> The mind cannot know;
> Follow your heart
> Wherever it wants to go.

KATIE.

> Lost in the night,
> You wonder what path to take
> 'Til a whisper comes through.

HILDA.

> Come out of the darkness
> Into the day!
> Your heart knows the way!
> Follow your heart.
>
> To the someone who needs you,
> As he did from the start,
> To the someone who waits for you
> To follow your heart.

(KATIE *and* HILDA *exit Left.*)

(The landscape-traveller opens on the Right. When half open, the LIGHTS come up behind it, revealing the kitchen of the Yoder home for Scene II.)

ACT TWO

Scene II

The kitchen of the Yoder home.

An old-fashioned wood-burning cooking range is Right. A table with a meat grinder is Center; a butter churn standing on a low stool is Left Center; and Left is a sink, with a water pump. Up Left is a corner cupboard, and across the back wall are other tables, cluttered with pots, bowls, a bread board, dishes, etc.

EMMA *and* FIVE AMISH WOMEN *are bustling about, cooking, stirring, slicing, etc.*

BESSIE. *(Taking a tray of cookies from oven and crossing Center with it)* Streusel Kuchen I think we'll have enough, Emma.

SARAH. *(Crossing from sink to stove with a large old-fashioned coffee urn)* You think?

BESSIE. Plenty. Ninety-two people you counted for the wedding, ain't, Emma?

EMMA. *(Grinding liver at the Center table)* Yah!

REBECCA. *(Rolling out shupp noodles on the bread board, up Right)* I heard Abraham Lapp and his cousins can't come.

EMMA. Oh! Then figure eighty-six.

RACHEL. *(Churning butter Left Center)* Don't forget Rebecca Mast and the kids.

EMMA. All right, ninety-one. The babies, too?

RACHEL. Sure!

EMMA. Ninety-eight! Make already for one hundred. What they don't fress up, we'll give to the pigs.

BESSIE. *(Has put down tray up Center and is crossing to pump to wash her hands)* Yah, Emma.

REBECCA. Esther, see if the sauerkraut ain't finished.

(ESTHER goes to the stove, stirs and tastes. RUTH enters, surveys the busy scene and moves to Center.)

SARAH. *(Up Center, tasting)* Needs more salt, the shmir-kase.

EMMA. Yah, yah!

REBECCA. *(Crossing to Center table for spoon, almost bumping RUTH)* Needs more water, the dough!

ESTHER. *(Crossing up Center for salt, then back to stove, each time avoiding a minor collision with RUTH)* The sauerkraut's coming good!

EMMA. Good, good!

(MARY *enters, carrying a huge side of raw beef. She crosses* RUTH *and puts it on the floor by the corner cupboard up Left.)*

RUTH. *(Watching the beef)* Looks like he had a bad night!

EMMA. *(Looks up from her grinding)* Hello, Miss Winters!

RUTH. *(Enthusiastically, to* EMMA) I heard there's a bit of cooking going on. I'd like to help.

EMMA. You want to help cook?

RUTH. Sure. What was that dish Mr. King enjoyed so much at lunch—schnitzel-something?

EMMA. Kassler-ripschen.

RUTH. That's it. How do you make it?

EMMA. Oh, I can't help show you now. We're too busy fixing for the wedding.

RUTH. *(Starts to cross to table up Right)* Well, let me help— maybe I can pick up a few pointers.

EMMA. Sure, then.

ESTHER. *(Stopping* RUTH) Miss, please—if you can fill this pail with water from the pump— *(Hands her the large urn.)*

RUTH. Glad to! *(Takes urn to the sink, puts it under the pump and jiggles the pump handle tentatively)* Nothing's coming out.

EMMA. Pump! Pump! It'll come out water.

RUTH. *(Pumping more vigorously, she turns to* RACHEL) I'd love to get one of these where it comes out Scotch.

(She laughs, but RACHEL *stares coldly. In a moment, water starts coming out.)*

Hey, it works! This is fun!

SARAH. *(At up Center table, stirring the smier kase)* Miss, there, on the stove, the big pot, the water is boiling?

RUTH. *(Goes to stove and lifts lid with a pot holder)* Yes, it is—

SARAH. It's for rice. So put in please, from the box rice.

RUTH. Happy to! *(She finds the rice on top of the stove shelf and pours in a little.)*

ESTHER. The pail is filled already once?

RUTH. *(Pouring in a little more rice)* Just a minute. I'm new at this.

EMMA. So pump, please! We need it quick!

RUTH. Okay! *(She pours in the whole cannister of rice and starts leisurely for pump.)*

EMMA. *(Impatiently)* Pump! Pump!

(RUTH runs to pump and starts to work.)

RACHEL. Ooh, I'm tired so!

RUTH. What's that you're doing?

RACHEL. Churning butter—for two hours yet!

RUTH. You must be exhausted. Here, let me do it—

RACHEL. Thank you. *(She immediately abandons the churn and busies herself at the table up Center.)*

(RUTH *churns.)*

ESTHER. *(Calling to* RUTH) The pail water! I need it for the potatoes!

EMMA. Pump! Pump!

RUTH. So sorry! *(She starts pumping and churning simultaneously, achieving a sort of rhumba motion with her body.)*

BESSIE. *(Over* RUTH'S *shoulder, on her way to the corner cupboard with cakes)* It's fun cooking by us, ain't?

RUTH. *(Working desperately)* This is more fun than basket weaving! *(She churns and pumps. Suddenly she notices that the expanding rice has raised the lid above the pot and is spilling over)* Er—Miss—Madam—the pot there!

(But EMMA *is on her way to the cupboard and the* OTHERS *are too busy to notice.* RUTH *crosses quickly to stove and, using a pot holder, pushes the lid down.)*

RACHEL. The butter ain't finished yet, Miss—

RUTH. *(Recovering from momentary fatigue)* Oh, the butter! *(Crosses and resumes churning.)*

ESTHER. Miss! The water, please!

RUTH. In a second! *(Goes to pump as* EMMA *crosses back to her grinding.)*

REBECCA. Emma, help me with the shupp-noodles!

EMMA. Oh, all right, then— *(To* RUTH) Miss, please, grind up please the last few pieces. If you're not busy.

RUTH. My pleasure! *(She grinds a little, then pumps, then churns. She notices that the lid of the rice pot has risen again, crosses desperately to stove and slams the lid back in place, using a pot holder.)*

(The WOMEN *are completely unaware of* RUTH'S *problem.)*

SARAH. Taste for me the smier-kase.

EMMA. Don't put too much salt.

BESSIE. *(At the corner cupboard)* Rebecca Mast is bringing more dishes?

EMMA. Yah.

    *(RUTH *has gone back to grinding and churning, churning and pumping water. She sees that the rice pot lid has risen again and starts for stove.* EMMA, *coming down to Center table for more ground liver and to substitute an empty plate, intercepts her.* RUTH *is sheepish and frantic.)*

Pump! Pump!

(RUTH *gives her a sickly smile and returns to churning and pump-ing. As soon as* EMMA *clears up to table up Center,* RUTH *rushes to the stove and claps an old-fashioned flat iron on the lid of the rice pot. Harried, but feeling that this will do it, she starts nonchalantly back to the pump.*)

ESTHER. *(To* RUTH, *impatiently)* The water, please!
RUTH. *(Rushing to the pump)* Coming!
RACHEL. The butter is made yet?
RUTH. *(To the churn)* In a jiffy!
EMMA. The liver, Miss!
RUTH. I'm with you! *(She starts grinding, managing two or three revolutions of the handle, when the rice pot explodes, spew-ing rice and lid and flat iron onto the stove and floor.* RUTH *looks at each of the accusing* WOMEN *in consternation, then affects a phoney calm)* You'll have to excuse me, ladies. I'm late for an ap-pointment—with a hat box. *(She makes a hasty exit.)*
SARAH. *(Going back to the churn)* The lady from New York, she ain't acquainted so good by the kitchen.
REBECCA. *(Cleaning up the mess at the stove)* But who cooks by her in the house? The husband?
BESSIE. She ain't got a husband.
EMMA. *(Crossing to down Center)* No wonder, the way she cooks! Bessie, go by the cellar and bring salt.
BESSIE. Yah, Emma. *(She exits.)*
EMMA. You see how it is with a city lady? Ach, they have such a sad life!
RACHEL. Maybe if we was city ladies, we would enjoy there?
EMMA. Enjoy? No, never!

*(SONG: "CITY MOUSE—COUNTRY MOUSE"—*EMMA, RA-CHEL, ESTHER, REBECCA, MARY AND GRETCHEN.)

EMMA.
> Once upon a time there was a country mouse,
> Paid a visit to her relative, the city mouse.
> But she didn't care a bit for her city mouse,
> And her heart was full of pity for the city mouse.
> I feel the same as she—
> A city mouse I'd never want to be!

*(*EMMA *and the* AMISH GIRLS *move into One,* GRETCHEN *bringing a collander with her as the LIGHTS brighten.)*

> City mouse, city mouse, full of care!
> What dress to buy? What dress to wear?
> Country mouse, country mouse, worries not:
> She wears the only one she's got!

ESTHER.
>City mouse, city mouse, fuss and fret!
>What should she be—blonde or brunette?

EMMA.
>Country mouse reckon a diff'rent way—
>She's happy if it don't turn gray!

RACHEL.
>The city mouse must always watch her figure!

EMMA.
>She better keep it slender if she's wise!
>It's different with the fellers in the country—
>They like the large economy size!

(She raises RACHEL's *hand in demonstration.)*

REBECCA.
>City mouse wonders what love's about.

4 GIRLS.
>She reads a book, to puzzle it out.

EMMA.
>Country mouse, country mouse, reads no book:
>She goes into the barn and takes a look!

(There is a simple dance routine. The bird-traveller closes easily behind them, and the rest of the number is in One.)

EMMA.
>City mouse tries to be brainy kind,
>Wants to be loved, just for her mind.
>Country mouse, country mouse, well aware
>What fellers want is not up there!

(She demonstrates, tapping forehead of GIRL *to her Right.)*

MARY.
>City mouse in such a stew,
>Raising one child, so hard to do!

EMMA.
>Country mouse, country mouse, she does fine!
>Number one takes care of number nine!

RACHEL.
>No complicated gadgets in the kitchen—

GRETCHEN.
>No complicated notions in the head—

EMMA.
>And when it's time for maybe getting married,
>No complications in the bed!

REBECCA.
> City mouse, city mouse, one fine day,
> Pack up your bag, tiptoe away!

EMMA.
> Look around till you've found a country—spouse!

(MALE *heads pop out from the stage Right portal, wearing alternately red and white nightcaps. The* BOYS *beckon the* GIRLS *off.*)

ALL.
> And settle down to be a country mouse!

(*The MUSIC comes to a finish, and the* AMISH GIRLS *make a character exit, Right, with* EMMA *wearing the collander like a helmet. The* BOYS *disappear with their beckoning gesture.*)

(*The bird-traveller opens on the back porch of the Yoder house, where* DAN *and* PAPA *are in negotiation over the River Farm, with* ISAAC *kibitzing.*)

ACT TWO

SCENE III

The back porch of the Yoder home.

This is a fold-out from a built flat, within the house portal. A stool is set by DAN *at Right of the railing, and he is seated on it as the bird-traveller opens.* PAPA *is standing Left of him,* ISAAC *at Right.*

PAPA. I tell you, Mister, forty-five hundred is a fair price.
ISAAC. Yah—is a good price.
DAN. *(Rising)* To tell you the truth, Mr. Yoder, someone else is interested in the property.
PAPA. For real?
DAN. Yes.
PAPA. *(After a pause)* Forty-*eight* hundred.
ISAAC. Is a good price!
DAN. I'll have to talk to this other person before I decide.
PAPA. An Amishman?
DAN. Yes.
PAPA. *(Crossing Left a step or two)* Five thousand.
ISAAC. Is a *good* price!
DAN. Mr. Yoder, I want to hear what this other fellow offers—
PAPA. *(Coming back to* DAN) What other fellow?

DAN. Peter.

PAPA. *(Angrily)* Peter! Mister, this is shreklich! A hexer, a sinful person, he wants only to hurt me with this talk of buying your farm.

DAN. He doesn't want to hurt you, Mr. Yoder. The barn was no more hexed than—

PAPA. *(Interrupting, facing* DAN) You want to sell your place or no?

DAN. I think you're being unfair to the boy. All I'm trying to do is—

PAPA. Don't try! Katie is going to marry Ezra. *(He crosses away, down Left)* Don't try nothing!

DAN. *(Crossing down to* PAPA; *deliberately)* Mr. Yoder, I had another offer for the land. For a good deal more money. I didn't consider it because I thought it would hurt you people. But maybe I was wrong.

ISAAC. Hurt? How, Mister?

DAN. This company wants to build a factory here.

PAPA. *(Turning to* DAN) A factory?

DAN. A paper box factory. There would be over a thousand workers, I imagine.

ISAAC. *(Crossing* DAN, *to* PAPA) City people!

PAPA. *(Pause, then furiously)* Do it then! Sell it to them! Bring in the strangers! Me you can't handle like this! *(He starts to exit Left.)*

ISAAC. *(Holds him back)* Jacob! Think once! Think what happened in Stultville. Bird-in-Hand will not be for us any more!

PAPA. Then we will go! Away!

ISAAC. Jacob! Your pride is worth more than everything?

(PAPA *looks at* DAN *bitterly, then exits down Left.)*

(ISAAC *turns to* DAN) Mister, such a thing you could not do!

DAN. *(Crossing on to porch, Right of door)* I don't want to hurt any of you. But I do want to help a boy who's in trouble. *(He sits on the railing and lights a cigarette.)*

HILDA. *(Enters from house and goes to* ISAAC, *Left of porch)* Papa, in the kitchen Mama wants you.

ISAAC. *(Preoccupied)* What?

HILDA. In the stove, the fire needs fixing.

ISAAC. All right. *(He crosses up to the door and stops)* Mister, you'll think on it, ain't?

DAN. I will. But I hope Mr. Yoder does some thinking too.

ISAAC. Yah. *(He exits glumly into the house.)*

HILDA. I'm happy you and Papa are friendly like.

DAN. He seems like a very nice man.

HILDA. Yah. We are all friendly here.

DAN. Are you?

HILDA. *(Crossing to Center)* Oh, sure. From us Amish came bundling.

DAN. Well, you can't get much friendlier than that!

HILDA. *(Smiles at him, sits on the stool. Pause)* Dan—

DAN. Yes, Hilda?

HILDA. I was happy like anything when you said I was a pretty one, and all like that.

DAN. Well, I meant it, Hilda. Every word of it.

HILDA. I know you did. I felt for sure you were not like making fun with me.

DAN. Of course not.

HILDA. Your grandfather was Amish, ain't?

DAN. Sure. Old Joshua Koenig.

HILDA. Koenig. I like the sound of it. Koenig.

DAN. It's King now. That's what it means, you know.

HILDA. I know. It fits you. It's strong-like. *(She looks at him)* I like you very much, Dan. More than any man around here, ever.

DAN. I like you too, Hilda.

HILDA. You do?

DAN. Very much.

HILDA. *(Rocking back and forth on the stool with pleasure)* Papa will be surprised to hear!

DAN. To hear what?

HILDA. Always he has said I am not for marrying!

DAN. *(Rising slowly, stunned)* Marrying—?

HILDA. *(Happily, not looking at him)* Oh, when Papa hears your name is really Koenig!

DAN. *(Coming off porch behind her and crossing slowly to Left)* Hilda!—

HILDA. *(Sincerely)* I will make you a good wife, Dan. Surely.

DAN. *(Not looking at her)* Hilda—sit down.

HILDA. *(Surprised)* I am sitting.

DAN. Oh, yes. Of course. *(Turning to her)* Hilda, you're an Amish girl. I'm a New Yorker. You could only be happy here.

HILDA. I could be happy any place, I think.

DAN. Hilda, please listen to me—

HILDA. Yes, Dan—

DAN. I said I like you. I do like you. Very much. You're a fine girl, a wonderful girl. But—that's all I meant, really.

HILDA. *(Puzzled and hurt)* You do not want marrying?

DAN. Hilda, it's impossible. Believe me, it wouldn't be fair to you.

HILDA. *(Realizes, in a dead voice)* You do not want marrying.

DAN. *(Crosses and kneels by her side, takes her hand; gently)* Please listen to me. You don't know me. You don't know how I live. You don't really know what it would be like to be away from here. Do you understand me?

HILDA. I understand only one thing clear. You do not want marrying.

DAN. Can't you see how wrong it is, Hilda? You'd be lost away

from here. We're as far apart as—as Bird-in-Hand is from New
York. I'm going back there in a day or two—
      (HILDA *sits quietly for a moment, then looks at him, and
      abruptly dashes off Right, in tears.*)
Now, wait! Hilda!

*(But she is gone. He looks after her, drops his cigarette and steps
on it, furious with himstlf. The landscape-traveller closes from
Right and* DAN *exits Left, encountering* THREE AMISH GIRLS
as he goes.)

      GIRL #1. *(Passing* DAN *to Right, who disregards her)* Hello,
Mr. King! That's him! That's the one Hilda's stuck on!
      GIRL #2. Him?
      GIRL #3. But he's not Amish even!
      GIRL #2. That Hilda!
      GIRL #3. She's getting to be a terrible wild one!
      GIRL #1. Should we tell her Papa?
      GIRL #3. No.
      GIRL #2. We ought to tell somebody!
      GIRL #1. Who?
      GIRL #2. Let's tell all the other girls!

*(They exit Right, giggling. The landscape-traveller opens to Left,
revealing* RUTH'S *little-room-under-the-stairs.)*

ACT TWO

SCENE IV

Ruth's room.

*(*RUTH *is at the bed, frantically trying to get her hat-box open, but
it is securely locked.)*

      RUTH. I never needed a drink this bad! *(She claws at the lock
with her nails)* Torn to shreds in an Amish kitchen! He's not worth
it! Ouch! *(She waves her finger in pain. She takes off a shoe and
starts hacking fruitlessly at the lock. She stops, throws shoe down,
pants heavily and stares at hat-box)* That dandy Mark Cross and
his dandy guaranteed locks! *(She goes to the dresser, looking for
the key)* That key must be here some place! *(She discovers a nail-
file and decides to try that. She pries at the lock, but it bends into
a horse-shoe shape. She looks at it and flings it on bed)* It's the
booze hex, that's what it is! I've got to get this thing open— *(She
crosses to the window and calls out)* You, there—you, hoo—could
you come up a minute? I need some help!

(She lights a cigarette, and is putting her shoe on when there is a KNOCK and EZRA *enters. He is uncomfortable, staring at her cigarette.)*

(RUTH *is Left of the bed*) Oh—this. Well, I'm a Baptist and we're allowed!—Ezra, could you give me a hand? See if you can get this hat-box open.

EZRA. *(Right of bed)* I'll try anyway. *(He tugs at the hat-box, but not very strenuously)* It's stuck.

RUTH. I know, dear. That's the problem.

EZRA. Let me try again. *(He picks it up, wraps his arms around it and tugs. The whole top breaks off and he puts it down on bed.)*

RUTH. You are a sturdy one! Thanks a lot. *(She goes to the hat-box for the bottle)* Er—sit down. *(She goes to dresser for a glass.)*

*(*EZRA *hesitates.)*

(Noticing EZRA'S *uncertainty)* Have a sitz!

*(*EZRA *crosses to the armchair and sits down. He stares at her as she pours a drink, and she becomes aware of the embarrassment.)*

Oh, we Baptists are a wild bunch! *(Then, in toast)* Gesundheit! *(She drinks, and sits comfortably on the chest at the foot of the bed, crossing her legs.)*

*(*EZRA *crosses his arms, which happens to show off his biceps.)*

Say, you do have muscles, don't you?

EZRA. *(Smiling)* I am maybe the strongest one around.

RUTH. *(Pouring another snort)* Congratulations!

EZRA. What is that?

RUTH. *(Putting the bottle on the floor between them)* Well—er—it's a tonic—sort of.

EZRA. For women's troubles?

RUTH. For women's troubles, men's troubles—anybody's troubles. It's made out of—er—er—vegetables.

EZRA. Vegetables—?

RUTH. Sure. You know—corn and rye and barley—stuff like that. Very good for the nerves.

EZRA. Oh! Well—today also I am a little nervous. With the barn burning, and my wedding tomorrow— *(He reaches for the glass.)*

RUTH. Oh, no! You're not that nervous! Let's just sit and talk a little.

EZRA. Talk?

RUTH. Yes— Well, Ezra, you're getting married tomorrow—

EZRA. Yah!—Maybe, could I taste the vegetable juice? *(He takes the glass out of* RUTH'S *hand.)*

RUTH. *(Protesting, but he has it)* Well—

EZRA. *(Sniffing drink, incredulous)* Vegetables?

RUTH. That's right!

EzRA. *(Slugs down the whole drink, and grasps his throat in burning surprise)* Vegetables?

RUTH. Well—ah—*old* vegetables! *(As* EzRA *settles back)* Now, we can talk.

EzRA. *(A broad grin lightens his face)* Yah!

RUTH. *(Sardonically)* Yah! I don't suppose you'd care for a cigarette, would you?

EzRA. *(Righteously)* Oh, no! Cigarettes are forbidden! *(He picks up bottle and pours another drink.)*

RUTH. *(Tries to stop him)* Now, wait a minute, please!

EzRA. *(About to drink, he stops to toast)* Gezundheit!

RUTH. *(Turning away, front)* That's your opinion!

EzRA. *(He slugs down the drink. It seems to have no effect. He puts glass down on the floor. Settling back in the chair)* Now we talk!

RUTH. Well, Ezra, what would you like to talk about?

EzRA. *(Happily dazed)* Yah!

RUTH. You said it! Well, now! Ezra, what kind of crops do you raise mainly?

Ezra. Crops? *(He giggles stupidly.)*

RUTH. Yes.

(No response but a giggle from EzRA.*)*

I guess I shouldn't have asked that. I barely know you!

(They BOTH *start for the bottle, but* EzRA *beats her to it.)*

Go ahead! Don't be shy!

(EzRA pours a drink and downs it. RUTH *finds the cork on the chest, caps the bottle, and crosses to put it on dressser.)*

EzRA. *(In a sudden loud voice)* My Uncle Albert died funny!

RUTH. *(At dresser)* What?

EzRA. He was plowing by the turnips, he came home for supper, all of a sudden he breathed hard-like, and then he died-like!

RUTH. *(Crossing in to Center)* That reminds *me* of a funny one! I have a little cousin—

(EzRA roars with laughter.)

You said it!

(There is a KNOCK at the door.)

Oh, my God! You can't be found here! You better get out of sight!—Come here— *(She pulls him, grinning happily, to the curtained-off corner of the room and pushes him into it.)*

(There is another KNOCK.)

Just a minute!—Coming!—

(EzRA stands grinning over the top of the curtains.)

(RUTH is frantic; moves the armchair up, out of the way) Just a minute! *(She pushes* EzRA *down into a sitting position)* Down, boy!

(Another KNOCK.)

(RUTH *is suddenly aware that* EZRA'S *feet are protuding from under the curtain. She tries to push them out of sight, fanny to the audience, then turns around, working laboriously)* Who is it?

HILDA. *(Outside)* Hilda! *(She comes in.)*

RUTH. Oh! What do you want, Hilda? *(She has* EZRA'S *shoes in her hands.)*

HILDA. *(To Center)* I want to see you a minute—

RUTH. *(As* HILDA *stares at* EZRA'S *feet)* Ahhh— My walking shoes—

HILDA. Miss Ruth, I want you should give me a cigarette!

RUTH. Sure, dear. *(She drops* EZRA'S *shoes, crosses* HILDA *toward dresser, suddenly does a double take)* What?

HILDA. I want to smoke and all! Like you!

RUTH. This whole community is falling apart! *(Takes* HILDA *by the shoulders)* What's the matter, honey?

HILDA. *(Tearfully)* What's the good to be Amish? I want to be like you—and him.

RUTH. Who?—Oh, you mean Dan?

HILDA. He is not for marrying a one like me. He said so.

RUTH. Marrying?

HILDA. I thought for sure he liked me. He said I was so pretty and all— And now— *(She starts to pace away, but notices* EZRA'S *feet sticking out from beneath the curtains. She pulls away the curtains, downstage to upstage, revealing* EZRA *sitting on the floor.)*

    (RUTH turns away, upstage, Right of the chair.)
Ezra! What are you doing there?

EZRA. Sitzing.

HILDA. Why are you sitzing?

EZRA. I'm tired!

HILDA. *(Taking glass and sniffing it)* Ezra—you're drinking schnapps! *(She gives the glass back to him.)*

EZRA. *(With a happy smile)* From vegetables!

HILDA. *(To* RUTH) What happened to him?

RUTH. *(Turning to* HILDA) Well, sir! We were sitting around telling funny stories—

HILDA. Ezra? He was never for fun!

EZRA. *(Rises from floor, crosses* HILDA *to Center)* Now I am for fun! You know what? Over by Lancaster, there is a carnival!

HILDA. So?

EZRA. So I'm going!

HILDA. Ezra! A carnival? With music and nokkid girls and gambling games? An Amish to go to such a place!

EZRA. *(Gleefully) Once!*

RUTH. Ezra! You're getting married tomorrow and—

EZRA. So I am going today! Anybody want to come with? Hilda—?

HILDA. *(Considering it, to herself)* To the carnival—?

RUTH. Hilda? She can't go to a place like that! *(Takes glass from* EZRA *and crosses to the dresser with it)* An Amish girl! What's the matter with you?

EZRA. So nobody's going? So goodbye, I'll come back later, when I'm here sometime. *(He lurches out the door.)*

RUTH. Wait a minute, Ezra! *(She follows him out.)*

HILDA. To the carnival? *(An idea forms in her mind.)*

(SONG: "I'LL SHOW 'IM"—HILDA.)

HILDA.
    Maybe he thinks I'm sitting in a corner,
    Sobbing like a ninny
    With my eyes all red!
    Or maybe he thinks I'm standing in the garden,
    Staring at his window,
    Wishing I was dead!

(She runs to the chest.)

    Well, he can just go and soak his head!

(She unhooks her blouse and takes it off.)

    I'll show him!
    I'll show him how little I care!
    When we meet I'll just stand with my nose in the air!

(She flings the blouse on to chair and crosses her arms.)

    Though he's sighing,
    And pleading and down on his knees,

(She points as if he were kneeling down Left.)

    I'll tell him I think he's full of cheese!

(She sits on the chest.)

    He can just save his breath!

(Takes off her Left shoe.)

    He can leave me alone!
    If he's starving to death,
    I won't throw him a bone.

(Puts on RUTH'S *Left red shoe.)*

    I'll show him
    How happy I am to be free
    Of a nothing who's nothing to me!

(She takes off her Right shoe, replacing it with a red one.)

    He'll find out I'm not yet such a baby!

(She stands, but her ankles buckle from the high heels and she
falls back.)

I'm all through with acting like a dunce!

(She rises again and wobbles Left.)

Any girl who thinks he's worth the having
Ought to have her head examined once!
He's too old for me—he must be fifty!
Any feller fifty is no prize!
Furthermore, his eyes are kind of shifty—
I don't trust a man with shifty eyes!

(She crosses up and gets black bra.)

I'll show him how easy he is to forget;

(Putting the bra on, well above her bosom.)

In a week I won't even remember him, yet!

(She pulls the bra even higher.)

I'll be flirting

(Gesture of flirting.)

With fellers I don't even know,
In—

(Hand to face in dismay.)

—wherever it is fellers go!

(She crosses up for red dress.)

Fancy dresses I'll wear,
Fancy pants underneath!

(Puts dress on bed, removes own skirt.)

Fine perfume in my hair,
And a rose in my teeth!

(She tosses her skirt away on chair.)

I'll show him!—the way he showed me—

(Putting on red dress over her head.)

What a smart girl a lummox can be—
Me he won't find sitting home and loafing!

(Gets fur piece, tries it around her neck, but is puzzled by the clip
mouth and decides this is wrong.)

I'll go places where I've never been!

(Tries the fur piece around her head, but rejects this too.)

Papa says by Lancaster is sinful—

(Clips fur piece to Left side of her bra and smooths it down with her hand.)

I'll go down to Lancaster and—sin!

(She makes a wide, sweeping gesture on the last word and runs out the door.)

(LIGHTS blackout.)

(The landscape-traveller closes to the Right. PETER comes on with it from Left, carrying a bench and a twig. He is seated, brooding, when the LIGHTS come up again.)

ACT TWO

SCENE V

In front of the landscape-traveller. PETER is seated on a bench, Left, which he sets for himself in the dark. He is holding a twig.

TWO AMISH BOYS *cross from Left to Right, ignoring* PETER. KATIE *enters from Right, crossing to* PETER.

PETER. *(Rising)* Katie, you should not have come by my house. Somebody will see you!

KATIE. I know it is wrong, but I could not help it. Only to say goodbye I came. Maybe I will not see you again, ever.

PETER. No, Katie. You will not see me again. Ever.

KATIE. Peter, my heart is hurt by your shunning. For loving me only you suffer.

(PETER turns away from her.)

Also, for loving you, I suffer—

PETER. Goodbye, Katie—

RUTH. *(Off Right)* Peter! *(Entering from Right)* Peter! Where's Ezra?

PETER. I have not seen him.

RUTH. Oh, fine. He really went to that carnival.

KATIE. Carnival? Ezra went to the carnival? He must be fericht!

RUTH. *(Crossing KATIE to PETER)* He's also a little plastered— Drunk! You ought to get him home, Peter.

PETER. *(He breaks the twig in agitation)* Let Katie's Papa bring him home!

RUTH. I hope nothing happens to him—the day before his wedding. It would be quite a scandal, wouldn't it?

PETER. Yah. *(He doesn't move.)*

RUTH. *(Crossing to Right)* —Maybe I can find Dan somewhere—

PETER. *(Looks at* KATIE*)* I will go!

(RUTH *stops and turns.*)

KATIE. Peter, it could only bring you more trouble!

PETER. He is yet my brother—and shame he must not bring on you!

KATIE. *(Stepping toward him)* Peter—you will come back—?

PETER. *(Tortured)* No, not ever! I will send Ezra back! *(He goes off Left.)*

RUTH. *(Going to* KATIE*)* Katie—

(KATIE *does not respond.*)

(RUTH *crosses to Right Center, turns, suddenly aware of the evening chill)* Katie, it's getting cool. Why don't you come into the house with me?

KATIE. *(Sitting on bench)* No, thank you. I will maybe stay here, and wait—a little.

(RUTH *goes off Right.*)

(REPRISE: "YOUNG AND FOOLISH"—KATIE.)

KATIE.

—Soon enough the carefree days,
The sunlit days go by.
Soon enough the bluebird has to fly.
We were foolish:
One day we fell in love.
Now we wonder
What we were dreaming of,
Smiling in the sunlight, laughing in the rain!
I wish that we were young and foolish again!

(She exits to Left as LIGHTS and MUSIC change. The landscape-traveller opens to Left, revealing the carnival midway.)

ACT TWO

SCENE VI

The midway on the carnival grounds in Lancaster.

Set pieces Right and Left advertise "Madam Zanda, the Human Pincushion" and "BoBo, the Dog-Faced Boy." BARKER #1 follows the traveller on from Right, bringing a stool to stand on BARKER #2, coming on from Left, uses the bench from the previous scene.

COUPLES *cross, gawking, flirting, thronging the scene as the* BARKERS *spiel.*

BARKER #1. *(Right)* All right! All right! Step right up, folks! See the ninth wonder of the world! Madam Zanda, the human pincushion! Right here, only a dime! The lady with the skin like rubber!

BARKER #2. *(Left)* All right, folks! Here y'are! See the most amazing, the most fantastic sight on earth! BoBo, the Dog-Faced Boy! Only a quarter, folks! BoBo, the boy with the face of a dog!

*(*BARKER #2 *exits Left, taking bench and picking up a* GIRL. MAMBO JOE *enters stage Left,* EZRA *from stage Right. They meet at Center.)*

EZRA. Hey, where do they sell here vegetable juice?

*(*MAMBO JOE *gives him a look and* EZRA *stumbles into the dance hall, the entrance to which is up Center.)*

GIRL. *(At Right after hearing* BARKER #1's *spiel)* I don't think it's possible to stick pins in a woman!
SAILOR. *(With her)* I'll take two!
BARKER #1. *(Ad lib)* Take your mother inside! *(He exits Right, clearing his stool.)*

*(*MAMBO JOE *begins a choreographed flirtation with* TWO FLOOZIES. HILDA *enters from Left, watching what is going on. When the* FLOOZIES *prance off Left,* HILDA *tries their technique with* JOE. *He responds, but finally frightens* HILDA, *who runs away, hiding behind set-piece Right Center.)*

(The set-piece, Right, is walked off as the MUSIC changes, revealing the booth of SCRANTON SALLY. *Very scantily clad, she performs a cooch dance on the platform as* TWO GRAPE GIRLS, *Right and Left of her, sing, scarcely heard because of the cat-calls and whistles of the on-lookers.)*

*(NUMBER: "SCRANTON SALLY"—*TWO GRAPE GIRLS.*)*

GIRLS.
        Scranton Sally!

What a dolly!
She can drive you
Off your trolley!
Tender-hearted, sympathetic,
Fond of fun and games—
And very ath-a-letic.
Every Tom and Dick and Harry,
From Altoona to Walkes-Barre,
Takes the train to Scranton frequently!
They don't come to see a movie,
Or the local musicale!
They want Scranton, Scranton, Scranton Sal!

(As SCRANTON SAL *finishes her dance, she fondles one of the on-lookers, and* HILDA *gets up on the platform, from behind. She is hooted at, and crosses in terrified confusion to the Left, where the set-piece has been walked-off, revealing the stand of* ATOMIC LOUIS.*)*

(The LIGHTS change, and ATOMIC LOUIS *is spieling.)*

ATOMIC LOUIS. Hurry, hurry, hurry! The Atomic Love Machine! Are you cold, lukewarm, hot, or sizzling? Are you sexy, sexy, sexy? Step right up, young lady! Don't be afraid to grab the handles, baby! They won't bite'cha!

(A GIRL *from the crowd grabs the handles and begins to shake in ecstasy. The pointer moves up and up. As it hits the top, LIGHTS flash on and the* GIRL *falls back into the arms of a spectator. Each of the* CROWD, *as he touches his neighbor, also shakes as if with electric shock.* HILDA *gets involved in this, and also* MAMBO JOE. *Finally the group breaks away and all but* JOE *enter the dance hall, carrying* HILDA *along with them.)*

*(*JOE, *searching for* HILDA, *exits Right, leaps back on again, tosses hat off Left and is Center as the LIGHTS come up behind the dance hall scrim. It flies out, revealing a wild* JOE, *with drunken* SPECTATORS, *including* EZRA, *seated at tables Right.)*

*(*HILDA *becomes involved in the dance as* JOE *pursues her. She is bumped by the dancers, crawls between their legs, etc.)*

*(*PETER *enters from down Left, looking desperately for* EZRA.*)*

(A SAILOR *makes a final eccentric pass at* HILDA, *and* JOE *finds her.* EZRA, *very drunk, finally sees her and tries to haul* JOE

away. JOE *flashes a knife and* EZRA *is too drunk to cope with him.* PETER *comes to the rescue, pulling* EZRA *away, where the* BOUNCERS *take charge of him, breaking* JOE'S *hold on the knife over his knee and knocking out another would-be battler.)*

(The tables are cleared, up, and the dance hall scrim flies in. Through the entrance door the BOUNCERS *fling* FIVE REVELLERS, *who roll into grotesque positions and lie still. The last of them is* MAMBO JOE, *who rolls erect, fists poised, then finally collapses, knocked out, as the MUSIC finishes.)*

(The landscape-traveller closes to the Right. EZRA *enters Left, his shirt torn, his hair rumpled, very drunk.* TWO AMISH WOMEN *in black capes and hoods come on from Right, bump into him at Left Center and exit Left in horror.* TWO AMISH GIRLS *come from Right, meet him Center, see his condition and exit Left, giggling at him.)*

(As EZRA *weaves to Right Center, the* TWO CHILDREN *come on from Right and see him, with horrified fascination.)*

YOUNG MILLER BOY. *Ezra!!*

(The CHILDREN *run off Right and* EZRA, *grabbing his head, staggers after them.)*

(The landscape-traveller opens to Right, revealing RUTH *putting down a pan of schnitz und knepp on a bench outside the Yoder kitchen, in One.)*

ACT TWO

SCENE VII

Outside the Yoder kitchen. The house portal, with plug.

RUTH *is discovered with a pan of schnitz und knepp, which she has just cooked. She places it on a bench and takes off her apron. She starts to pace, looking off in both directions.*

DAN. *(Entering from Right, crosses to Left of bench)*
    *(*RUTH *is Left.)*
Any sign of them?
    RUTH. *(Crossing in to Center)* No.
    DAN. I told you to leave that bottle in the car!
    RUTH. I didn't force it on him. He was nervous.

DAN. If Papa Yoder finds out about this Amish delegation to a carnival—

RUTH. He knows— I told him.

DAN. You told him? What did you do that for?

RUTH. Why not? Let him know that Peter went there to help his brother! After what he did to the poor kid— Let him think about it a little!

DAN. What did he say?

RUTH. He stared at me for a few minutes, and I left. *(She crosses to Left, looking off.)*

DAN. *(Also looking off Left)* Still no sign of them. *(He absently tastes from the dish)* Mmmmm—taste this!

RUTH. *(Crossing Right Center)* I did.

DAN. Great, isn't it?

RUTH. It's horrible! *(She crosses to far Right.)*

DAN. Kassel ripschen.

RUTH. *(Looking off Right)* Schnitz und knepp.

DAN. Oh? Wonderful flavor they get with that paprika!

RUTH. Garlic!

DAN. These apples are mashed or shredded or something.

RUTH. *(Turning to DAN)* No, first you dice them and then you— *(She stops.)*

DAN. *(Looks at her)* Then you what?

RUTH. *(Crossing to Center)* Forget it!

DAN. Ruth! You made this kassel ripshen!

RUTH. *(Crossing to Left)* Schnitz und knepp! *(She turns to DAN)* They've been gone an awfully long time.

DAN. *(Facing her)* Why did you make this, Ruth?

RUTH. Do me a favor and forget it. I apologize.

DAN. You made it because you knew I liked it.

RUTH. *(Looking away)* No, I didn't. Don't be maudlin.

DAN. I think you did.

RUTH. *(Crossing in to Center, bursts out)* All right, I made it because you liked it!

DAN. Ruth!

RUTH. And if you want to know why I went skiing with you last winter and almost broke my back, it's because you were on a skiing binge! And that damn duck hunting kick you were on! I almost froze standing up to my elbows in that miserable swamp!

DAN. Honey!

RUTH. Well, here's your beloved schnitz und knepp. *(She crosses away to Right)* But when you go in for parachute jumping, you jump alone!

DAN. *(Going to her, her back to him)* Ruth!

RUTH. Oh, stay away from me!

DAN. *(He is behind her)* I never realized that—it just never occurred to me that—you really made this?

RUTH. Oh, you're a boob!

DAN. I guess I am. *(Turning her around)* I mean, I was. *(He draws her to him and they kiss, lightly at first, then warmly.)*

RUTH. *(Nestling her head against his shoulder)* And every year I'll make schnitz und knepp for you—on Eric von Stroheim's birthday. *(Remembering)* Darling, what about Hilda?

DAN. Oh—yeah.

RUTH. What are you going to do about it, Dan?

DAN. I don't know. I was just being friendly and—

RUTH. I know, I know.

DAN. I still don't know what happened. She met someone wearing a collar and tie, and—I don't know *what* happened.

RUTH. Dan, you'll have to talk to her.

DAN. I tried! But what will I tell her? Maybe we can—

RUTH. *(Sees HILDA entering from Left, pushes DAN away)* You, Dan. I don't wear a collar and tie.

DAN. Hilda! What happened to you?

HILDA. *(Crossing DAN to Center. She is bedraggled, having lost her shoes and fur piece)* I was by the carnival.

DAN. What made you do that?

(HILDA *doesn't answer.*)

Hilda, that was very foolish.

HILDA. No. I wanted to see different people than I live with always. And I *saw!* They made me afraid!

DAN. I'm sorry, Hilda.

HILDA. I do not know these people—just like you said. I do not know you, even.

DAN. That's right.

HILDA. Coming back, I asked myself—who are these people? Who is this Dan? Neat he is, and polite, and with shiny shoes. But a girl does not marry shiny shoes, ain't?

DAN. Of course not.

HILDA. *(To RUTH)* Different he is from the men around here, but is he better? *(To DAN)* Excuse me, *that* I do not know.

DAN. Of course. And there must be some very nice men here.

HILDA. Surely. And younger, too. So I will look, and I will find him, ain't?

(RUTH *crosses in to* HILDA.)

(SONG: "TAKE YOUR TIME AND TAKE YOUR PICK"— RUTH, DAN, AND HILDA.)

RUTH.
While looking around for that fortunate man,
One little word of warning from Aunt Ruth—
DAN.
And Uncle Dan.

RUTH.
Take your time—
DAN.
And take your pick!
RUTH.
Till you find the one designed to be your pick!
DAN.
Never trust that first impression when a feller comes to call.
RUTH.
As a matter of fact, you're wiser never trusting him at all.
DAN.
Look around before you leap.
Though the ways of modern scientists are deep—
RUTH.
They ain't found a way to tell a good man from a creep.
BOTH.
So take your time and take your pick!
HILDA.
I'll take my time and take my pick,
Till I'm sure beyond all cure that he's my pick!
He'll be handy in the barnyard, with the cattle and the sheep.
RUTH.
He'll be handy on the sofa, when the sheep have gone to sleep.
DAN.
But though his build seems early Greek,
RUTH.
Though his monumental shoulders turn you weak,
DAN.
Is it nature or the tailor gave him that psysique?
Take your time—
RUTH.
And take a peek!
DAN.
Take your time, and take your pick.
Pick too quick and what a pickle you can pick!
There's the kind of man who dazzles you with conversation bright.
RUTH.
Then you marry the guy and all he says is, "What's to eat tonight?"
DAN.
So pick your time, and time your pick.
RUTH.
Don't just marry any Harry, Tom, or Dick!
DAN.
You can end up with no paddle up that famous creek!
BOTH.
So take your time and take your pick!

(RUTH and DAN do a simple vaudeville dance step, which HILDA

*tries to imitate. The bird-traveller closes behind them. As the
dance steps get a little more complicated,* HILDA *gives up and
does a joyous folk dance turn across stage to Right.)*

HILDA.
I'll take my time, and take my pick!
Till I pick the one who'll stick through thin and thick.
At a party he won't notice when the pretty girls arrive—
    RUTH.
If you ever find a man like that, make sure he's still alive!
    DAN.
So take your time,
    RUTH.
Not too much time!
Don't delay until you're way beyond your prime—
They won't let you be so picky when you're old as I'm—
    BOTH.
But take your time, and take your pick—
    DAN.
Till you find the one it's fun to dance with, chick-to chick!
    RUTH.
Who will never spike the shoo-fly pie with arsenic!
    HILDA.
I'll just look and look until I find the perfect—Zook!
    ALL 3. Take your time, and take your pick!

*(As the MUSIC finishes, they take each other's hands in a three-
way handshake.*

*(The bird-traveller opens behind them on the applause, and they
step back into the Yoder yard.)*

ACT TWO

SCENE VIII

*The bird-traveller opens on the Yoder yard. It is early morning,
and during the scene the LIGHTS brighten gradually as the
sun rises.*

    MILLER CHILDREN. *(Dashing across from Left and into house)*
Uncle Jacob— Uncle Jacob!

*(EZRA staggers on from down Left, dishevelled and holding his
head.)*

RUTH. *(Seeing* EZRA, *from Right Center)* Look what's coming by the road over once!

DAN. *(Going to* EZRA *and catching him as he trips)* Ezra! What happened?!

HILDA. *(Clearing up Left Center with* RUTH) If Uncle Jacob knows he was by the carnival, it will be terrible around here!

DAN. Let's get him cleaned up a little!

KATIE. *(Entering from the house)* Ezra! Where is Peter?

EZRA. *(Befuddled)* He was going some place, I think.

PAPA. *(Coming on to porch with the* MILLER CHILDREN)
     (KATIE *moves Right, on porch, the* CHILDREN *Right and Left.)*
Ezra! You was at the carnival!

EZRA. It was not plain vegetable juice!

(He exchanges a look with RUTH, *who then looks at* DAN *and retires to above the wagon.* HILDA *sits on the Center of the wagon, watching.)*

PAPA. You sinned like this?

EZRA. But I didn't start the fighting— *(He sprawls on the porch steps.)*

PAPA. Fighting, also! The day before your wedding! And drunk yet! Look at you! Fighting and drinking in an evil place!

EZRA. I will be all right for the wedding.

PAPA. There will be no wedding! My girl will not marry such a one!

EZRA. But my whole family is coming!

PAPA. Everybody is coming! But I will have to send them away. Such a shame I never had yet! *(To the* CHILDREN) Go into the house, children.

(They do. EZRA *stumbles off Right in Two as* PETER *enters down Left with a* STATE TROOPER, *who pushes him in to Center.)*

KATIE. Peter!

HILDA. A policeman yet!

DAN. *(Left of the* TROOPER) What's the trouble, Officer?

TROOPER. This fellow was creating a disturbance at the carnival.

DAN. Now look, Officer—

TROOPER. I would have taken him in, only I figured I'd give him a break this one time.

PAPA. Why did you bring him here like this?

TROOPER. *(Crossing* PETER *to Right Center)* Look, Mister, we never had any trouble with any of you people before, but this was a real brawl! There were five guys laid out cold.

DAN. But he didn't start it, did he?

TROOPER. I don't care who started it—he did his share. And he didn't even want to come back. I had to drag him.

PETER. *(Crosses away to Left, after a look at* KATIE) No, I did not want to come back.

(RUTH *crosses in Left Center.)*

TROOPER. One more word out of you and I will take you in!

PAPA. *(Coming down off porch)* For what, Mister?

TROOPER. For what! For creating a disturbance, like I said. What was he doing in a place like that anyway?

DAN. He didn't go there to make trouble, Officer—

PAPA. I heard why he went. I've been thinking why he went.

TROOPER. He had no business being there.

PAPA. He went by that place to help his brother only. His brother was making trouble, not him! To save his brother from shame he went there. To save us all from shame.

TROOPER. Look, all I know is—

PAPA. Know better that sometimes people punish too fast, without thinking a little. It was a hard thing Peter did—and a good thing!

TROOPER. Well, as long as he behaves himself— *(He exits down Left in One.)*

DAN. *(Following him to down Left)* Everything will be all right, Officer. Thanks a lot!

PETER. *(Crossing in to Right Center)* Mister Yoder—

PAPA. Yah?

PETER. Everybody is coming to a wedding to your house— You should have a wedding for them, ain't?

KATIE. *(Going to* PETER) Always we have wanted marrying, Papa.

DAN. They only want what you want, Mr. Yoder. A good Amish marriage, and a good Amish family. Besides, Peter's a man of property now. I'm selling him the River Farm.

PAPA. Katie, I always wanted what is good for you.

KATIE. I know, Papa.

PAPA. Maybe I made mistakes! *(Turns to* DAN) It is like my grandfather always said— We grow too soon old, and too late schmart! *(He pats* PETER'S *shoulder in blessing.)*

(PETER *and* KATIE *embrace.)*

RUTH. *(Crossing to* DAN, *Center)* Dan, I think we'd better get going.

DAN. All right. Goodbye, Hilda—

(But HILDA *is absorbed with a young* AMISHMAN, *who is hanging over the downstage end of the wagon.)*

RUTH. Leave her alone. She's working.

PAPA. *(As* DAN *and* RUTH *start to go)* Mr. King, stay at least for the wedding.

DAN. We'd love to.

EMMA. *(Coming from house with a wedding cake)* Look at this! The wedding cake for Katie and Ezra!

HILDA. *(Crossing to Right Center)* No, Emma! Katie and *Peter!*

EMMA. Katie and *Peter!*

(FINALE REPRISE: "PLENTY OF PENNSYLVANIA"—
THE COMPANY.)

EMMA.
> This is all very new to me!
> Knocks me right off my feet!

HILDA.
> Peter's getting her,
> Papa's letting her—

ALL.
> We got anyway plenty to eat!

(MUSIC segue into "Plenty of Pennsylvania" as EMMA *shows wedding cake to* COUPLES *Right.)*

> Plenty of Pennsylvania!
> You've never seen the likes of

(Two YOUNG AMISHMEN *come on from Left with gaily-painted dowry chest, which they place Center.* EMMA *puts the cake on it.)*

> Plenty of Pennsylvania—
> Where anything grows!

*(ANOTHER AMISHMAN *brings on an old-fashioned wooden armchair from Left, places it Center, beside chest.* PETER *makes* KATIE *try it, rocking her.)*

ALL.
> Plenty of Pennsylvania!

(Two AMISH GIRLS *bring on a handsome tub from Left, place it Left of chest and take up positions sitting beside it on floor.)*

> No pastures green the likes of
> Plenty of Pennsylvania—
> Where anything grows!

*(THREE AMISH GIRLS *dance on with a gaily-colored Pennsylvania Dutch quilt held between them. They circle around Right and stand with the quilt in front of them.)*

All you need is some seed and a plow or two,

(ANOTHER AMISH GIRL *carries on a footstool to match the rocker and places it in front of the chair.*)

And a bull who's keeping company with a cow or two:

(SAMUEL *carries on a baby's cradle, which he puts in front of* KATIE *and* PETER, *who react suitably.*)

Soon you've got

(DAN *steps forward and gives* PETER *the deed to the River Farm.*)

> Plenty of Pennsylvania!
> Sweet land of meadows golden,
> And fat red barns for holdin'
> What goes to town on market day!
> Plenty of! Plenty of! Plenty of everything,
> In Pennsylvan-i-ay!

(The HOUSE CURTAIN drops on the end of the play. The MUSIC immediately picks up with "Young and Foolish" for the curtain calls.)

(The first curtain call finds the PRINCIPALS *lined up across stage, above the wedding presents, the* CHORUS *grouped around and behind them. This is a company call.)*

(The second curtain call goes up on the company in the same positions, and remains up while the PRINCIPALS *step down and back for bows in the following order:* JACOB *and* ISAAC; EZRA *and* EMMA; PAPA *and* SAMUEL; PETER *and* KATIE; DAN, RUTH *and* HILDA.)*

(The HOUSE CURTAIN remains up. On the last notes of "Young and Foolish," the map scrim flies in, and ALL *sing "It Wonders me," seen through the scrim.)*

ALL.

> It wonders me,
> It wonders me,
> So beautiful a day can be!
> So green the field,
> So blue the sky,

(The LIGHTS fade out behind the scrim and come up in front of it, so that the whole scene fades from view.)

> So gold the tree!
> It wonders me!

(Only the map scrim can be seen. The house curtain comes in.)

HOUSE LIGHTS

PLAIN AND FANCY

LINE PLOT

From Curtain Line			
	Number of		
Feet	Inches	Lines	Name of Pieces
	6	5	#1 Portal
1		5	Portal Elect
1	6	5	Portal Masking
2		5	Map Drop
3		5	Elect Cross Over
3	6	5	#1 Elect Xrays
4		5	#2 Elect Spots
5	6	7	#1 Traveler
6		5	Black Out Drop
6	6	7	#2 Traveler
8		7	House Portal Fly
9		5	#3 Elect Xrays
10	6	5	Straight Border
11		5	Barn Landscape Drop
11	6	5	Shunning Leg Drop
12		5	Carnival Scrim
12	6	5	#2 Portal Border
13		2	#2 Portal Legs
13	6	5	#4 Elect
14		5	Elect Cross Over
14	6	3	Parlor Flat
15	6	5	Crystal Ball
16	6	5	#3 Portal Border
17		5	#5 Elect Xrays
17	6	2	#3 Portal Legs
18	6	5	Dance Pavilion Leg Drop
19		5	Shunning Scrim Drop
19	6	5	Green Drop
20		5	#6 Elect Proj.
21		5	Gas Station Drop
21	6	5	Yoder Tree Drop
22		5	#4 Portal Border
22	6	5	Dance Pavilion Drop
23		6	#4 Portal Legs
24		5	#7 Elect Xrays
25		5	Yoder Yard Drop
26	6	5	#8 Elect
28		5	Sky Drop

85

PROP LIST

Scene 11—Gas Station Drop
    Automobile
    3 green vegetable crates (strong enough to stand on)
    Chamber pot with lid
    Prop plucked chicken with head (rubber)
    Book
    Glasses with ribbon
    Pennsylvania road map
    Space cadet helmet
    Panda doll 2' tall
Scene 12—Full Stage with Tree Drop
    Amish buggy, with reins, but no shafts
    4 grass or hay rakes
    Cultivating rake
    2 hoes
    3 large market baskets
Scene 13—Landscape Traveller
    Green bench 3'6" long. Long batten pin-hinged to its end, so
        it can be pushed on from wings
    Extra large market basket, loaded with vegetables, brown
        paper sacks, etc.
    Letter in envelope
Scene 14—Full Stage Yoder Farm Yard
    2 benches 6' long
    Bench 4'6" long
    Platform 5' x 2' x 10"
    Apple butter churn
    Prop fire for churn to sit on
    2 saw horses 29" high, 36" long
    Table-top 9' x 3'
    Crate 24" x 14" (strong enough to stand on)
    Low florist crate containing geraniums in pots
    Wagon—flat—patform wagon, 7' x 3' plus wheels (chocks
        for wheels)
    5 large bags of meal or feed
    Bushel basket of prop apples
    Bushel basket of prop tomatoes
    Large basket of prop potatoes
    Tall basket with 12 ears of prop corn, loose
    2 large pumpkins
    4 wicker cornucopies filled with Fall flowers
    X-type saw horse

Log partly sawed through
Buck saw
Long pole to stir apple butter
Snow pusher to scoop up fire
Large wooden bowl with real apple and chopper
4 small wooden bowls each with apple and paring knife
4 copper cooking pots each with potato and paring knife
2 prop apples
Embroidered and fringed cloth which hooks to table top, making an apron around the ends and front

Scene 15—Inset—Yoder Parlor
Long settle
2 simple chairs
4 pegs on wall with prop hats
Wall mottoes, calendar, etc.
Wall magazine rack
Man's suitcase
Woman's hatbox
Large prop cabbage with yellow edges

Scene 16—Behind Yoder House
Same as used in Scene 13
Copy book with blue bird painted on cover

Scene 17—Barn Drop
8' ladder has hooks on it for hanging lanterns
Paint can
Paint brush

Scene 18—Ruth's Bedroom
Washstand, with scarf, drinking glass, oil lamp with base that can be used as ash tray
Towel rack and towel mounted on D.S. end of washstand
Bed with sheets, pillow and pillow case, patchwork quilt
Small chest at foot of bed
Armchair
Roller shade on window
Curtains to close off corner of room. Must be free moving on a pole and shoulder high for Ruth
Hooks on battens, mounted where convenient on wall
Wooden tub 24" across, 12" deep
Cigarettes and lighter
Bottle of Scotch
Hat box as used in Scene 15 containing red dress, skirt, pair panties, fur neck piece, dressing gown, lace bra, pair bedroom slippers (Note: bra and fur neck piece in side pocket of hat box)

Scene 19—Yoder Yard: Barn Burning and Shunning
(Main props same as Scene 14)
4 low stools
2 bean bags

Soft ball
8 wedding presents, assorted sizes, wrapped in white
3 folding chairs
Lunch pail
5 shallow wicker baskets, various sizes
2 prop axes
10 buckets
Horse collar
(Rakes, feed sacks, etc., double from previous scenes)

Scene 21—Full Stage—Barn Raising

Table top 2' x 3' (sets on sawhorses from Scene 14)
Nail keg
Clean pail with ladle
8 small pails 6" high
9 hammers
2 block planes
2 paint brushes
Cross cut saw
Spoke shave
2 zig-zag rules
5 screw drivers
Tray with metal pitcher of water and 5 glasses
Corn broom
Cookies in two shallow baskets from Scene 19
8' step ladder
2 16' platform ladders
Weather vane on end of pole, with fittings to hook over top
    of finished barn

Scene 22—Inset—Yoder Kitchen

Stove with trick rice pot
Table 42" x 25"
Table 6' x 20"
Table 3' x 18"
Kitchen sink with practical pump
Corner cupboard
Butter churn bolted to low stool
Shelf on wall with fake clock
Kitchen match holder on wall by stove
Side of raw beef
2 copper cooking pots
Dish pans with real potatoes
Large bowl, full of darkened pop-corn
Breadboard with rubber dough rolled out
Rolling pin
China canister of rice
Wooden salt box
Large coffee urn to fill with water
Meat grinder

Wooden flat iron
12 assorted plates dinner size
Tray of cookies to fit in oven
Several pot holders
6 large wooden spoons
Collendar big enough to fit on Emma's head
4 dish towels
2 paring knives
2 large kitchen knives
Spatula
Heaping plate of bologna to be ground up

Scene 23—Back Porch
Low stool (double from Scene 19)
Cigarettes and lighter

Scene 24—Bedroom
Furniture same as Scene 18
2 plastic glasses
Trick nail file
Red dress hanging on hook next to window
Pair red shoes at foot of bed
Scotch bottle

Scene 25—Landscape Traveller
Green bench (double from Scene 13 without batten)
Twig (broken each performance)

Scene 26—Carnival and Dance Hall
2 low stools for barkers (double from earlier scenes)
6 wire ice cream chairs
2 wire ice cream tables
Several plastic glasses
Leather imitation knife 8" long
Calling cards
2 cloth imitation black jacks

Scene 27—Back of Yoder House
Bench (double from previous scene)
Pan of cookies

Scene 28—Yoder Yard—Finale
Basic props same as Scene 14)
Wedding cake
Rose (Ruth)
Dowry chest, handle at both ends
Rocking chair
Milking stool
Large tub
Cradle
Patchwork quilt
Legal paper (deed to farm)

PLAIN AND FANCY

COSTUME SCENES CHART

ACT ONE

DANCER
(Jeff Duncan) 9

Scene 11
White turtle neck sweater, black slacks
   rolled up
White sox and sneakers
Scene 14
Pa. costume, brown shoes & sox. Fall
Scene 17
Barn-raising costume, blue trousers
Vest, shirt
Scene 19
Same as 14—Plain We Live blue barn
   raising costume
Inside Yoder Barn Scene
Same as Plain We Live
Fire crossover—hat and coat off—
   sleeves rolled up

DANCER
(Crandall Diehl) 6

Scene 14
Pa. costume—brown shoes & sox. Fall
Scene 17
Barn raising costume—blue trousers—
   vest & shirt
Scene 19
Same as 14. Not in Plain We Live
Inside Yoder Barn Scene
Same as 14. Fire cross over—hat and
   coat off, sleeves rolled up

DANCER
(Ronnie Lee) 7

Scene 11
SWING BOY—green slacks & turtle
   neck sweater
Brown shoes and sox
Scene 14
Pa. Costume, shoes same as 11. Straw
   hat—Fall
Scene 19
Not in Plain We Live
Inside Yoder Barn Scene
Same as 14—fire cross over—hat and
   coat off
Sleeves rolled up

90

DANCER (Robert St. Clair 8	*Scene 11* Black slacks, bright blue sweater coat trimmed in white, pink T shirt— Brown shoes and sox *Scene 14* Pa. costume, shoes same as 11, Fall *Scene 17* Barn raising costume, blue trousers Vest and shirt *Scene 19* Same as 14—Plain We Live—blue barn raising costume *Inside Yoder Barn Scene* Same as Plain We Live—fire crossover Hat and coat off—sleeves rolled up
DANCER (David Wood) 9	*Scene 11* Powder blue slacks, green bright shirt corduroy Brown shoes and sox *Scene 14* Pa. rostume, shoes same as 11, straw hat, Fall *Scene 19* Same as 14. Not in Plain We Live *Inside Yoder Barn Scene* Same as 14—fire cross over, hat and coat off, sleeves rolled up
BESSIE (Faith Daltry) Singer 1	*Scene 11* White felt skirt, blue jersey blouse, black pumps, opera length net stockings *Scene 14* Pa. costume, brown shoes *Scene 19* Same as 14 *Inside Yoder Barn Scene* Same as 14
GRETA (Renee Orin) Singer 2	*Scene 11* Black and white striped blouse, black skirt, kerchief around head, fusia, black pumps, O.L. hose *Scene 12* Pa. costume (quick change on stage) *Scene 14* Pa. costume, brown shoes Same as 14 *Scene 19* Same as 14

Inside Yoder Barn Scene

ESTHER
(Sybil Lamb)
Singer   3

Scene 11
Black slacks, black and white jersey
  blouse, red belt, black flats, O.I..
  hose natural color
Scene 12
Pa. costcme (quick change on stage)
Scene 14
Pa. costume, brown shoes
Scene 19
Same as 14
Inside Yoder Barn Scene
Same as 14

REBECCA
(Betty McGuire)
Singer   4

Scene 11
Black pleated skirt, white blouse,
  green scarf for neck, black pumps
Scene 12
Pa. costume (quick change on stage)
Scene 14
Pa. costume, brown shoes
Scene 19
Same as 14
Inside Yoder Barn Scene
Same as 14

MARY
(Muriel Shaw)
Singer   5

Scene 12
Pa. costume (quick change on stage)
Scene 14
Pa. costume, brown shoes
Scene 19
Same as 14
Inside Yoder Barn Scene
Same as 14

SINGER
(Martha Flynn)   6

Scene 11
White and black polka dot skirt, black
  jersey blouse, pink scarf, black
  pumps, O.L. hose
Scene 14
Pa. costume, brown shoes (business)
Scene 19
Same as 14
Inside Yoder Barn Scene
Same as 14

SINGER
(Suzanne Easter)   7

Scene 11
Black and white circular skirt, purple
  blouse, red scarf, black pumps, O.L.
  hose
Scene 12
Pa. costume (quick change on stage)

			Scene 14
			Pa. costume, brown shoes
			Scene 19
			Same as 14
			Inside Yoder Barn Scene
			Same as 14
SINGER			*Scene 11*
(Betty Zollinger)	8		Black skirt, black and white slipover blouse, yellow scarf, black pumps, O.L. hose
			Scene 12
			Pa. costume (quick change on stage)
			Scene 14
			Pa. costume, brown shoes
			Scene 19
			Same as 14
			Inside Yoder Barn Scene
			Same as 14
SINGER	9		*Scene 19*
			Same as 14
			Inside Yoder Barn Scene
			Same as 14
DANCER			*Scene 11*
(Sara Aman)	1		Black skirt, pink blouse, blue scarf, black pumps, opera length hose
			Scene 14
			Pa. costume, brown shoes
			Scene 17
			Barn raising costume
			Scene 19
			Same as 14
			Inside Yoder Barn Scene
			Same as 14
DANCER			*Scene 11*
(Cathy Conklin)	2		Black pedal pushers, white jersey and black bolero, orange scarf, black flats, white wool sox
			Scene 14
			Pa. costume, brown shoes
			Scene 19
			Same as 14
			Inside Yoder Barn Scene
			Same as 14
DANCER			*Scene 11*
(Imelda DeMartin)	3		Black pleated skirt, white sailor blouse, black tie, black flats, white sox

Scene 14
Pa. costume, brown shoes
Scene 19
Same as 14
Inside Yoder Barn Scene
Same as 14

DANCER
(Ina Hahn) 4

Scene 11
Bright blue skirt, yellow jersey blouse, black pumps, opera length hose
Scene 14
Pa. costume, brown shoes
Scene 17
Barn raising costume, blue dress, apron, white cap
Scene 19
Same as 14
Inside Yoder Barn Scene
Same as 14

DANCER
(Lucia Lambert) 5

Scene 14
Pa. costume, brown shoes
Scene 17
Barn raising costume
Scene 19
Same as 14
Inside Yoder Barn Scene
Same as 14

DANCER
(Joan Darby) 6

Scene 11
Black short pants, knee length black plaid argyle sox, black jacket, white blouse, black flats, O.L. hose
Scene 14
Pa. costume, brown shoes
Scene 19
Same as 14
Inside Yoder Barn Scene
Same as 14

DANCER
(Diana Hunter) 7

Scene 11
Black gab skirt, striped blouse, black bolero, rainbow scarf, black pumps, O.L. hose
Scene 14
Pa. costume, brown shoes
Scene 19
Same as 14
Inside Yoder Barn Scene
Same as 14

DANCER
(Ann Needham)   8   *Scene 11*
Black jumper dress, torquoise jacket, black pumps, opera length hose
Scene 14
Pa. costume, brown shoes
Scene 17
Barn raising costume, blue dress, apron, white cap
Scene 19
Same as 14
Inside Yoder Barn Scene
Same as 14

DANCER
(Beryl Towbin)   9   *Scene 11*
Black skirt, orange blouse, black bolero, overblouse, black pumps, O.P. hose
Scene 14
Pa. costume, brown shoes
Scene 19
Same as 14
Inside Yoder Barn Scene
Same as 14

RUTH
(Shirl Conway)   1   *Scene 11*
Black satin sailor hat, black gloves, 3 chain plain gold choker and bracelet, black shoes, black purse, fur mink stole, net stockings—tan, blue aqua dress, wool jersey, piece—dummy zipper sewed on left side of dress, large earrings
Scene 13
Same as 11
Scene 14
Same as 11
Scene 15
Same as 11
Scene 18
Same as 11—fur stole on bed—no hat, red dress, purple skirt, pink shoes and panties, pink robe, black bra and neck piece and black panties, white half slip, pink bra

DAN
(Richard Derr)   2   *Scene 11*
Sport coat, plain, 2 shades of tan, grey flannel slacks, tan shoes, navy blue socks, maroon tie, white shirt
Scene 13
Same as 11

Scene 14
Same as 11
Scene 15
Same as 11
Scene 16
Same as 11
Scene 17
Same as 11
Scene 18
Same as 11
Scene 19
Same as 11
Inside Yoder Barn Scene
Same as 11
Fire crossover coat off, shirt collar
open, tie loosened

KATIE
(Gloria Marlowe)   3

Scene 12
Blue dress, grey apron, grey shawl,
charcoal bonnett and shawl, black
Amish shoes, black hose
Scene 14
Same as scene 12, without bonnett and
shawl
Scene 15
Same as 14
Scene 16
Same as 14
Scene 17
Same as 14
Scene 19
Same as 14
Inside Yoder Barn Scene
Same as 14

PAPA
(Stefan Schnabel)   4

Scene 12
Black suit, grey vest, fall and chin,
black overcoat and hat, black high
shoes
Scene 15
Same as 12, no coat or hat, sleeves
rolled up
Scene 16
Same as 15—with hat and coat
Scene 19
Same as 15
Inside Yoder Barn Scene
Same as 15—fire cross overcoat and
hat off, sleeves rolled up

ISAAC
(Sammy Smith)   5

Scene 13
Grey hat, black pants-shirt-vest, fall and chin piece, black shoes, brown sox
Scene 15
Same as 13—no hat or coat
Scene 16
Same as 15

EMMA
(Nancy Andrews)   6

Scene 14
Pa. costume, tan, black shoes, black hose
Scene 19
Same as 14
Inside Yoder Barn Scene
Same as 14

EZRA
(Douglas Rodgers)   7

Scene 14
No hat, pants, shirt, army buckskin shoes
Scene 15
Same as 14
Scene 19
Same as 14
Inside Yoder Barn Scene
Same as 14

HILDA
(Barbara Cook)   8

Scene 14
Pa. costume, blue, high black shoes, black hose
Scene 15
Same as 14
Scene 16
Same as 14
Scene 18
Same as 14
Scene 19
Same as 14
Inside Yoder Barn Scene
Same as 14

BOY
(Scotty Engel)   9

Scene 11
Dark blue dungarees, white T-shirt, brown oxford shoes, brown sox, space helmet
Scene 14
Straw hat, Pa. costume, tan brown oxford shoes and sox
Scene 15
Same as 14
Scene 18
Same as 14

Scene 19
Same as 14
Inside Yoder Barn Scene
Same as 14

GIRL
(Elaine Lynn)   10   *Scene 11*
Black velvet skirt, white blouse, shell rim glasses, panda bear, black shoes and sox
Scene 14
Pa. costume, tan brown shoes and stockings
Scene 15
Same as 14
Scene 18
Same as 14
Scene 19
Same as 14
Inside Yoder Barn Scene
Same as 14

PETER
(David Daniels)   11   *Scene 14*
Brown trousers, tan shirt and vest, hat, brown shoes and sox
Scene 15
Same as 14
Scene 17
Blue trousers, blue shirt, brown shoes and sox
Scene 19
Same as 17
Inside Yoder Barn Scene
Same as 17

RACHEL
(Ethel M. Cody)   12   *Scene 11*
Grey dress, washable, black shoes
Scene 14
Pa. costume, black shoes and stockings
Scene 19
Same as 14 with black bonnet and shawl
Inside Yoder Barn Scene
Same as 14

SAMUEL ZOOK
(Daniel Nagrin)   *Scene 14*
Black pants, grey shirt, light blue vest, black hat, black shoes
Scene 17
Barn raising costume, light grey shirt, blue vest, blue trousers
Scene 19
Same as 14

Inside Yoder Barn Scene
Same as 14, no hat and sleeves rolled up for fire crossover

SINGER-ANOTHER
MAN-SAMUEL LAPP
(Chris Robinson) 1

Scene 11
Black gab. slacks, red and white plaid shirt, brown oxford shoes and sox

Scene 14
Brown felt hat, Pa. costume, shoes same as 11, fal and chin

Scene 15
Same as 14—green coat and brown hat

Scene 19
Same as 15—Plain we live—blue barn raising costume

Inside Yoder Barn Scene
Same as Plain We Live; fire crossover, hat and coat off, sleeves rolled up

SINGER—A MAN
ABNER ZOOK
(James Schlader) 2

Scene 11
Black and white plaid jacket, back gab. slacks, yellow turtle neck sweater, brown shoes and socks

Scene 12
Pa. costume (quick change on stage)

Scene 14
Felt hat, Pa. costume, shoes same as 11, fall and chin

Scene 15
Same as 14—coat and hat

Scene 19
Same as 14, Plain We Live—blue barn raising costume

Inside Yoder Barn Scene
Same as Plain We Live—fire crossover, hat and coat off, sleeves rolled up

JACOB YODER
(Will Able) 14

Scene 14
Pa. costume, brown shoes and sox, felt hat—Fall

Scene 15
Same as 14—coat and hat

Scene 19
Same as 14

Inside Yoder Barn Scene
Same as 14

MOSES ZOOK
(Edgar Thompson)
Singer 3

Scene 11
Black slacks, black and white windbreaker, pink shirt, brown shoes and sox

Scene 12
Pa. costume (quick change onstage)
Scene 14
Pa. costume, shoes same as 11, Fall
Scene 15
Same as 14—coat and hat
Scene 19
Same as 14—Plain We Live, blue barn
raising costume
Inside Yoder Barn Scene
Same as Plain We Live—fire crossover,
hat and coat off, sleeves rolled up

ABNER ZOOK
(Tim Scheeretts)
Singer   4

Scene 11
White coveralls, cotton black-white
plaid shirt, colored handkerchief,
brown shoes and sox
Scene 14
Pa. costume, business straw hat, chin
and fall, shoes same as 11
Scene 15
Same as 14—coat and hat
Scene 19
Same as 14—Plain We Live, blue barn
raising costume
Inside Yoder Barn Scene
Same as Plain We Live—fire crossover,
hat and coat off, sleeves rolled up

AN AMISHMAN
(Herbert Surface)
Singer   5

Scene 11
Business suit, oxford brown shoes and
sox, black homburg, shell rim glass-
es, white shirt and black bow tie
Scene 12
Pa. costume (quick change on stage)
Scene 14
Pa. costume—Falls—shoes same as 11
Scene 19
Same as 14—Plain We Live—blue
barn raising costume
Inside Yoder Barn Scene
Same as Plain We Live—fire crossover,
hat and coat off, sleeves rolled up

STATE TROOPER
(Ray Hyson)
Singer   6

Scene 11
White coveralls, colored handkerchief,
grey plaid shirt, brown shoes and
sox, blue peak cap
Scene 14
Straw hat, chin piece, Pa. costume,
Fall—straw, shoes same as 11

Scene 19
Same as 14—Plain We Live, blue barn
    raising costume
Inside Yoder Barn Scene
Same as Plain We Live—fire crossover,
    hat and coat off, sleeves rolled up

SINGER
(Jack Irwin)   7
Scene 11
Black slacks, black and white T shirt
    under a pink shirt, brown shoes and
    sox
Scene 12
Pa. costume, quick change
Scene 14
Pa. costume, Fall—shoes same as 11
Scene 19
Same as 14—Plain We Live—blue barn
    raising costume
Inside Yoder Barn Scene
Same as Plain We Live—fire crossover,
    hat and coat off, sleeves rolled up

SINGER
(Robert Kole)   8
Scene 11
Black slacks with white inserts on side,
    yellow corduroy shirt, brown shoes
    and sox
Scene 12
Pa. costume (quick change on stage)
Scene 14
Pa. costume, Fall—shoes same as 11
Scene 19
Same as 14—Plain We Live, blue barn
    raising costume
Inside Yoder Barn Scene
Same as Plain We Live—fire crossover,
    hat and coat off, sleeves rolled up

SINGER
(John Sheehan)   9
Scene 14
Pa. costume—Fall, brown shoes and
    sox
Scene 19
Same as 14—Plain We Live—blue barn
    raising costume
Inside Yoder Barn Scene
Same as Plain We Live—fire crossover,
    hat and coat off, sleeves rolled up

SINGER
(Paul Brown)   10
Scene 14
Pa. costume—Fall—brown shoes and
    sox

Scene 19
Same as 14—Plain We Live—blue barn
    raising costume
Inside Yoder Barn Scene
Same as Plain We Live—fire crossover,
    hat and coat off, sleeves rolled up

LEVI STOIZFUSS
(William Weslow)
Dancer   1

Scene 11
Black gab. slacks, black and white
    leather zip. windbreaker, white navy
    cap, brown shoes and sox
Scene 14
Pa. costume—Fall—shoes same as 11
Scene 19
Same as 14—Plain We Live—blue barn
    raising costume
Inside Yoder Barn Scene
Same as Plain We Live—fire crossover,
    hat and coat off, sleeves rolled up

IKE PILERSHEIM
(James S. Moore)
Dancer   2

Scene 11
Black slacks, black and white turtle
    neck sweater, jockey cap, brown
    shoes and sox
Scene 14
Pa. costume, straw hat, shoes same as
    11—Fall
Scene 15
Same as 14—coat and hat
Scene 19
Same as 14—not in Plain We Live

ANOTHER AMISHMAN
(Robert Lindgren)
Dancer   3

Scene 11
Turtle neck sweater, black, white and
    yellow—black slacks—naval officer
    cap, brown shoes and sox
Scene 14
Pa. costume—shoes same as 11—Fall
Scene 19
Same as 14—Plain We Live—blue barn
    raising costume
Inside Yoder Barn Scene
Same as Plain We Live—fire crossover,
    hat and coat off, sleeves rolled up

DANCER
(Philip Nasta)   4

Scene 11
Black slacks, black red and white cot-
    ton shirt, brown shoes and sox
Scene 14
Pa. costume—shoes same as 11—Fall

Scene 19
Same as 14—Plain We Live—blue barn raising costume
Inside Yoder Barn Scene
Same as plain we live—fire crossover, hat and coat off, sleeves rolled up

ACT TWO

RUTH
(Shirl Conway)   1

Scene 21
Pink two piece jersey dress, pink kid shoes, two pink kerchiefs sewed together, tan net stockings, gold bracelet and earrings
Scene 22
Same as 21
Scene 24
Same as 22
Scene 25
Same as 24
Scene 28
White dress, jersey trimmed in red, red shoes, pumps
Scene 29
Same as 28

DAN
(Richard Derr)   2

Scene 21
Same as 19—no tie, shirt collar open
Scene 23
Tweed jacket, grey slacks
Scene 28
Sand gabardine suit, brown shoes, white shirt, maroon tie
Scene 29
Same as 28

KATIE
(Gloria Marlowe)   3

Scene 21
Cherry pink dress, white apron and cap, same shoes and stockings as in Act One
Scene 25
Same as 21
Scene 29
Same as 21

PAPA
(Stefan Schnabel)   4

Scene 21
Same as 16—no coat, wears hat
Scene 23
Same as 16
Scene 29
Trousers, vest, shirt

		Scene 21
ISAAC		Same as 13—no coat, wears hat
(Sammy Smith)	5	*Scene 23*
		Same as 15, no hat
		Scene 29
		No coat
EMMA		*Scene 21*
(Nancy Andrews)	6	Blue Pa. costume, same shoes and stockings as in Act One
		Scene 22
		Same as 21
EZRA		*Scene 21*
(Douglas Rodgers)	7	Same as Act One—wears hat
		Scene 24
		Same as Act One—no hat
		Scene 26
		Same as 24
		Scene 27
		Torn shirt—quick change
		Scene 29
		Same as 27
HILDA		*Scene 21*
(Barbara Cook)	8	Pink dress, white apron and cap, same shoes and stockings as in Act One
		Scene 23
		Same as 21
		Scene 24
		Same as 21—black bra, black panties, red satin shoes, red dress, fur neck piece
		Scene 26
		Red dress, red shoes, fur neck piece attached to dress
		Scene 28
		Same as 26—no shoes
		Scene 29
		Same as 26—no shoes
BOY		*Scene 27*
(Scotty Engel)	9	Same as Act One
		Scene 29
		Same as Act One
GIRL		*Scene 27*
(Elaine Lynn)	10	Same as Act One
		Scene 29
		Same as Act One
PETER		*Scene 21*
(David Daniels)	11	Brown trousers and tan shirt

Scene 25
Same as 21
Scene 26
Same as 25
Scene 29
Same as 26—torn shirt

RACHEL
(Ethel M. Cody)   12   *Scene 21*
Blue Pa. costume
Scene 22
Same as 21
Scene 27
Blue Pa. costume, black bonnet and
shawl
Scene 29
Blue Pa. costume

SAMUEL ZOOK
(Daniel Nagrin)   13   *Scene 21*
Same as 17 with hat
Scene 26
Mustard and green striped suit, blue
pancake hat, black shirt with laven-
der collar and orange tie, lavender
shoes, blue sox
Scene 27
Turbin with beard
Scene 29
Black hat, light blue pants—same as
17

JACOB YODER
(William Able)   14   *Scene 21*
Same as Act One
Scene 26
Powder blue sailor suit, brown shoes
Scene 29
Same as Act One

SAMUEL LAPP
ANOTHER MAN
(Chris Robinson)
Singer   1   *Scene 21*
Blue Pa. costume
Scene 26
Pink corduroy shirt, light brown trous-
ers, grass green sport coat, brown
henna hat, wears coat in Mambo
only
Scene 27
Barker in midway line
Scene 29
Same as 14

MOSES ZOOK
A MAN   *Scene 21*
Blue Pa. costume

(James Schlader) Singer	2	*Scene 26* Blue sport coat, purple pants, green jersey sweater *Scene 27* Not in midway *Scene 29* Same as 14
ABNER ZOOK (Edgar Thompson) Singer	3	*Scene 21* Blue Pa. costume *Scene 26* Powder blue suit, white, red and black checkered vest, wears coat in Mambo only *Scene 27* Barker in midway—Bouncer in dancehall *Scene 29* Same as 14
ABNER ZOOK (Tim Worthington) Singer	4	*Scene 21* Blue Pa. costume *Scene 26* Grey suit, grey and green plaid shirt *Scene 27* Bouncer in dancehall—same in midway *Scene 29* Same as 14
AN AMISHMAN (Herbert Surface) Singer	5	*Scene 21* Blue Pa. costume *Scene 26* Henna suit with white stripes, black turtle neck sweater *Scene 27* In dancehall only *Scene 29* Same as 14
STATE TROOPER (Ray Hyson) Singer	6	*Scene 21* Blue Pa. costume *Scene 29* State Trooper uniform
SINGER (Jack Irwin)	7	*Scene 21* Blue Pa. costume *Scene 26* Light blue slacks, apple green shirt *Scene 27* Dance hall only *Scene 29* Same as 14

SINGER		*Scene 21*
(Robert Kole)	8	Blue Pa. costume
		Scene 26
		Grey putty color suit with white stripes, yellow shirt
		Scene 27
		Midway and dance hall
		Scene 29
		Same as 14
SINGER		*Scene 21*
(John Dennis)		Blue Pa. costume
(Jack Sheehan)	9	*Scene 26*
		Blue sailor suit
		Scene 27
		Midway and dance hall
		Scene 29
		Same as 14
SINGER		*Scene 21*
(Paul Brown)	10	Blue Pa. costume
		Scene 22
		White night shirt and cap
		Scene 29
		Same as 14
LEVI STOLZFUSS		*Scene 21*
(Wm. Westlow)		Blue Pa. costume
Dancer	1	*Scene 22*
		White night shirt and cap
		Scene 26
		Grey suit, green jersey sweater
		Scene 27
		Dance hall
		Scene 29
		Same as 14
IKE PILERSHEIM		*Scene 21*
(James S. Moore)		Blue Pa. costume
Dancer	2	*Scene 26*
		Henna brown suit, green shirt
		Scene 27
		Dance hall
		Scene 29
		Same as 14
ANOTHER AMISHMAN		*Scene 21*
(Robert Lingren)		Blue Pa. costume
Dancer	3	*Scene 26*
		Black spangled in red robe, pink turban with pink feathers, red corduroy pants, lavender shirt

		Scene 27
		Fortune teller, dance hall, orange windbreaker
		Scene 29
		Same as 14
CAPTAIN		Scene 21
(Philip Nasta)		Blue Pa. costume
Dancer	4	Scene 26
		Black pants, orange, green and black plaid shirt
		Ear phone headgear, electrical wires
		Scene 27
		Dance hall—Barker love machine
		Scene 29
		Same as 14
DANCER		Scene 21
(Jeff Duncan)		Blue Pa. costume
(Saint Amant)	5	Scene 22
		Red night shirt
		Scene 26
		Light blue sport coat, gold shirt
		Scene 27
		Dance hall
		Scene 29
		Same as 14
DANCER		Scene 21
(Crandall Diehl)	6	Blue Pa. costume
		Scene 26
		Purple red slacks, lavender shirt, gold satin windbreaker
		Scene 27
		Dance hall
		Scene 29
		Same as 14
DANCER		Scene 21
(Ronnie Lee)	7	Blue Pa. costume
		Scene 22
		Red night shirt
		Scene 26
		Yellow slacks, rose shirt, green satin windbreaker
		Scene 27
		Midway and dance hall
		Scene 29
		Same as 14
DANCER		Scene 21
(Robert St Clair)	8	Blue Pa. costume

Scene 26
Grey suit, pink shirt
Scene 27
Dance hall
Scene 29
Same as 14

DANCER
(David Wood)   9

Scene 21
Blue Pa. costume
Scene 26
Light green slacks, light green jersey,
   2 tone blue jacket
Scene 27
Midway—dance hall
Scene 29
Same as 14

BESSIE
(Faith Daltry)
Singer   1

Scene 21
Blue Pa. costume
Scene 22
Same as 21
Scene 26
Royal blue dress with sequins, blue
   satin shoes, blue coat
Scene 27
Midway—dance hall
Scene 29
Same as 21

SAHARA
(Renee Orin)
Singer   2

Scene 21
Blue Pa. costume
Scene 22
Same as 21
Scene 23
Blue Pa. costume
Scene 26
Green aqua dress with sequins, pumps
   to match
Scene 27
Dance hall
Scene 29
Same as 21

ESTHER
(Sybil Lamb)
Singer   3

Scene 21
Blue Pa. costume
Scene 22
Same as 21
Scene 23
Blue Pa. costume
Scene 27
Blue Pa. costume for 27

			Scene 29
			Same as 21
REBECCA			*Scene 21*
(Betty McGuire)			Blue Pa. costume
Singer	4		*Scene 22*
			Same as 21
			Scene 23
			Blue Pa. costume
			Scene 26
			Green spangled Leartot, green spangled streamers, grapes on bra, headdress green leaves with grapes
			Scene 27
			2 tone red sequin dress, skirt, black pumps for both fast change
			Scene 29
			Same as 21
MARY			*Scene 21*
(Muriel Shaw)			Blue Pa. costume
Singer	5		*Scene 22*
			Same as 21
			Scene 26
			Same as Betty McGuire
			Scene 27
			Yellow dress with sequins, black pumps for both
			Blue Pa. costume
			Scene 29
			Same as 21
SINGER			*Scene 21*
(Martha Flynn)			Blue Pa. costume
(Marylin Bradley)	6		*Scene 26*
			Two tone red dress with sequins, black pumps
			Scene 27
			Midway, dance hall
			Scene 29
			Same as 21
SINGER			*Scene 21*
(Suzanne Easter)			Blue Pa. costume
(Janet Hayes)	7		*Scene 26*
			Pink dress with gold sequins, black pumps
			Scene 27
			Dance hall, blue Pa. costume
			Scene 29
			Same as 21

SINGER		*Scene 21*
(Betty Zollinger)	8	Blue Pa. costume
		Scene 26
		Yellow dress with sequins, yellow shoes
		Scene 27
		Midway—dance hall
		Scene 29
		Same as 21
SINGER	9	
DANCER		*Scene 21*
(Sara Aman)	1	Blue Pa. costume
		Scene 26
		Net bra with red poppies, flesh panties, rose panels with red sequins, black net hose, acqua shoes
		Scene 27
		Rose garter with red sequins, red poppies in hair, acqua blue dress with sequins
		Scene 29
		Same as 21
DANCER		*Scene 21*
(Cathy Conklin)		Blue Pa. costume
(Marsha Howard)	2	*Scene 26*
		Purple two tone dress, purple and blue sequins, flower in hair, green nile coat
		Scene 27
		Midway—dance hall
		Scene 29
		Same as 21
DANCER		*Scene 21*
(Imelda DeMartin)	3	Blue Pa. costume
		Scene 26
		Two tone red dress with sequins, hair up in ribbons, pony tail, yellow coat
		Scene 27
		Midway—dance hall
		Scene 29
		Same as 21
DANCER		*Scene 21*
(Ina Hahn)		Blue Pa. costume
(Nancy Lynch)	4	*Scene 26*
		Two tone red dress with sequins, red coat
		Scene 27
		Midway—dance hall

Scene 29
Same as 21

DANCER
(Lucia Lambert)   5   *Scene 21*
Blue Pa. costume
Scene 26
Rose dress with white dots, elbow gloves,
    small hat with feather, rose shoes
Scene 27
Midway—dance hall
Scene 29
Same as 21

DANCER
(Joan Darby)   6   *Scene 21*
Blue Pa. costume
Scene 26
Nile green dress with net sleeves, green
    hat with feathers, green shoes, green
    elbow gloves
Scene 27
Midway—dance hall
Scene 29
Same as 21

DANCER
(Diana Hunter)
(Tao Strong)   7   *Scene 21*
Blue Pa. costume
Scene 26
Purple dress with heavy fringe skirt,
    purple shoes, purple coat
Scene 27
Midway—dance hall
Scene 29
Same as 21

DANCER
(Ann Needham)   8   *Scene 21*
Blue Pa. costume
Scene 26
Navy blue dress with sequins, blue
    coat, blue shoes
Scene 27
Midway—dance hall
Scene 29
Same as 21

DANCER
(Beryl Towbin)
(Beverly Tassoni)   9   *Scene 21*
Blue Pa. costume
Scene 26
Deep red dress with sequins, fringe
    bottom, red shoes, yellow coat
Scene 27
Midway—dance hall
Scene 29
Same as 21

GAS STATION DROP

NO.3 PORTAL

NO.2 PORTAL

CRATE

NO.1 PORTAL

CAR

CRATE

CURTAIN LINE

ACT I - SCENE 1

SKY DROP

HILL GROUND ROW ELECTRIC

PORTAL

TREE DROP

PORTAL

BUGGY

PORTAL

PORTAL

ACT I - SCENE 2

SCENE DESIGNS

"PLAIN AND FANCY"

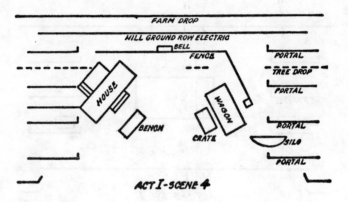

ACT I - SCENE 4

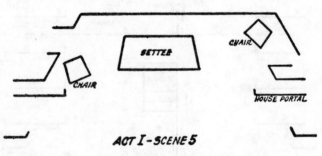

ACT I - SCENE 5

SCENE DESIGNS
"PLAIN AND FANCY"

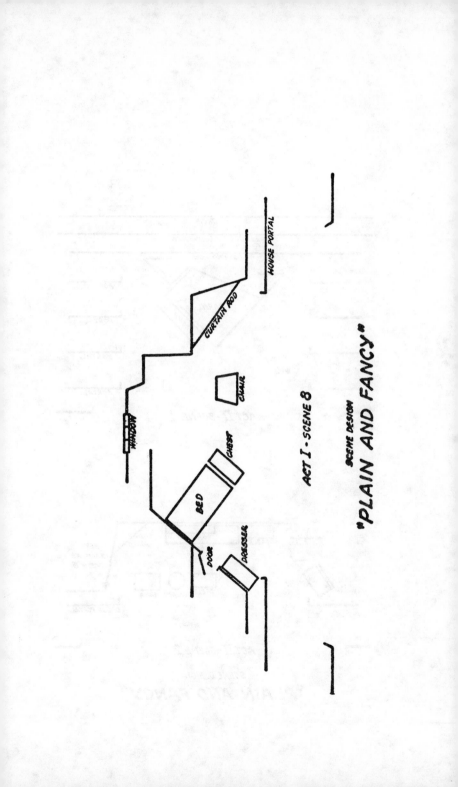

SCENE DESIGN

ACT I - SCENE 8

"PLAIN AND FANCY"

HOUSE PORTAL

CURTAIN ROD

WINDOW

CHAIR

CHEST

BED

DOOR

DRESSER

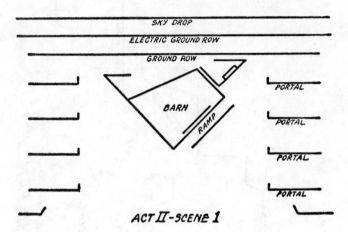

SKY DROP

ELECTRIC GROUND ROW

GROUND ROW

BARN

RAMP

PORTAL

PORTAL

PORTAL

PORTAL

ACT II - SCENE 1

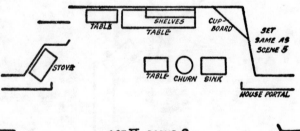

TABLE

SHELVES

TABLE

CUP-BOARD

SET SAME AS SCENE 5

STOVE

TABLE

CHURN

SINK

HOUSE PORTAL

ACT II - SCENE 2

SCENE DESIGN

"PLAIN AND FANCY"

Going Ape

NICK HALL

(Little Theatre.) Farce.

3 male, 2 female—Interior

This hilarious and almost indescribable farce has some serious undertones. Rupert, an idealistic and romantic young orphan, has come to his uncle's house to commit suicide. This proves to be no easy matter. For one thing he is constantly attended by his uncle's attractive nurse/secretary. He is also constantly interrupted by a stream of visitors, at first fairly normal, but increasingly incredible. Rupert realizes that all the visitors are the same three people, and his attention is drawn toward understanding the preposterously Victorian plot in which he is trapped, and which, in a startlingly theatrical climax, he begins to understand. "An intricate plot with subtle foreshadowing and a grab bag of surprises . . . some of the funniest characters you'll ever see molded into a tight dramatic package."—News, Fort Myers. "Every scene transcends not only the imagination, but melds into a literally death-defying whole. It's fast, like 2,000 mph . . . a play as old and as contemporary as today." Sarasota Journal. "Going Ape is truly zany . . . the wackiness is infectious." —Time.

(Royalty, $50-$25.)

Eat Your Heart Out

NICK HALL

(Little Theatre.) Comedy.

3 male, 2 female—Interior

In this theatrical comedy Charlie, an out of work actor currently employed as a waiter, takes the audience through a sequence of hilarious encounters in a succession of Manhattan restaurants. By changing the tablecloths during the course of the action the basic setting of three tables and six chairs becomes a variety of New York restaurants, both elegant and shabby. The scenes change, the action is uninterrupted and the comedy never stops. The other performers play several parts: the girl desperately trying to eat snails and oysters to please her fiance; the middle-aged couple whose marriage is breaking up; the lovers so intent on each other they cannot order dinner; the rich, embittered astrologer; the timid man who never gets a waiter; the agents, directors, actors, and waiters. An amusing gallery of characters whose stories intertwine and finally involve Charlie. The author of "Accommodations" has written a very funny, contemporary play that is also a serious comedy of backstage life. ". . . a sharp, stunning play. It'll make you howl—but better yet, it might even make you sniffle a bit."—Fort Lauderdale News. "Tightly written and very, very entertaining. I recommend it enthusiastically."—Miami Herald. ". . . About as good as anything I've ever seen in dinner theater . . ."—Fort Lauderdale Times.

(Royalty, $50-$25.)

The Gingerbread Lady

NEIL SIMON
(Little Theatre) Comedy-Drama
3 Men, 3 Women—Interior

Maureen Stapleton played the Broadway part of a popular singer who has gone to pot with booze and sex. We meet her at the end of a ten-week drying out period at a sanitarium, when her friend, her daughter, and an actor try to help her adjust to sobriety. But all three have the opposite effect on her. The friend is so constantly vain she loses her husband; the actor, a homosexual, is also doomed, and indeed loses his part three days before an opening; and the daughter needs more affection than she can spare her mother. Enter also a former lover louse, who ends up giving her a black eye. The birthday party washes out, the gingerbread lady falls off the wagon and careens onward to her own tragic end.

"He has combined an amusing comedy with the atmosphere of great sadness. His characteristic wit and humor are at their brilliant best, and his serious story of lost misfits can often be genuinely and deeply touching."—N.Y. Post. "Contains some of the brightest dialogue Simon has yet composed."—N.Y. Daily News. "Mr. Simon's play is as funny as ever—the customary avalanche of hilarity, and landslide of pure unbuttoned joy . . . Mr. Simon is a funny, funny man—with tears running down his cheek."—N.Y. Times.

Royalty $50-$35

The Sunshine Boys

NEIL SIMON
(All Groups) Comedy
5 Men, 2 Women

An ex-vaudeville team, Al Lewis and Willie Clarke, in spite of playing together for forty-three years, have a natural antipathy for one another. (Willie resents Al's habit of poking a finger in his chest, or perhaps accidentally spitting in his face). It has been eleven years since they have performed together, when along comes CBS-TV, who is preparing a "History of Comedy" special, that will of course include Willie and Al—the "Lewis and Clark" team back together again. In the meantime, Willie has been doing spot commercials, like for Schick (the razor blade shakes) or for Frito-Lay potato chips (he forgets the name), while Al is happily retired. The team gets back together again, only to have Al poke his finger in Willie's chest, and accidentally spit in his face.

". . . the most delightful play Mr. Simon has written for several seasons and proves why he is the ablest current author of stage humor."—Watts, N. Y. Post. "None of Simon's comedies has been more intimately written out of love and a bone-deep affinity with the theatrical scene and temperament." Time. ". . . another hit for Neil Simon in this shrewdly balanced, splendidly performed and rather touching slice of the show-biz life."—Watt, New York Daily News. "(Simon) . . . writes the most dependably crisp and funny dialogue around . . . always well-set and polished to a high lustre."—WABC-TV. ". . . a vaudeville act within a vaudeville act . . . Simon has done it again."—WCBS-TV.

Royalty $50-$35

THE LADY WHO CRIED FOX!!!
(LITTLE THEATRE—COMEDY)
By EDWARD CLINTON

3 men, 2 women—Interior

When a jealous actor who's always on the road, finds out his wife has taken on a young male roommate to meet expenses, the show does not go on. He immediately returns home to find out what's going on. The roommate, an inventor who likes to roller skate, is caught in the middle between a jealous husband and frustrated wife. Eventually, all five of the characters get into the act and the result is just plain fun. ". . . punch and humor . . . a funny play. . . ." — Miami Herald. ". . . clever script . . . intriguing sense of humor coupled with a powerful knack for drama. . . ." —Fort Lauderdale News. ". . . funny, delightful and above all devoid of the off color material so many writers feel is essential. . . ." —Hollywood, Fla. Sun Tattler.

(Royalty, $50-$35.)

NOT WITH MY DAUGHTER
(LITTLE THEATRE—COMEDY)
By JAY CHRISTOPHER

3 men, 3 women—Interior

Will Gray suddenly has a problem. His 18-year-old daughter appears at his "swinging singles" apartment door. It seems Will and his neighbor, Rip Tracy, a velvet-voiced radio Dee Jay have a penchant for juggling girls like antacid tablets. Poor Will has a go-go girl in the living room—with her motor running—and a devoted young lady in the bedroom—but that's o.k. since she loves him. Rip has a girl in his apartment already when Will calls on him to also entertain the go-go girl. Then Will's daughter appears to complicate matters further—not only are explanations in order—but daughter has problems of her own. How it all is resolved will leave the audience limp with laughter. An adult play with not one leering joke. It's all in fun. "Funny? Absolutely." —High Point, N.C. Enterprise. ". . . a laugh riot . . ." —Greensboro, N.C. Daily News. ". . . fast-paced farce with as many laughs as you can handle in one sitting." —Lexington, Ky. Herald.

(Royalty, $50-$25.)

POOR BITOS

By JEAN ANOUILH, *translated by* LUCIENNE HILL

DRAMA

10 males, 3 females, 1 child—Interior

The French master of time and its illusions presents us in his latest play
with a group of patricians gathered for a party in the vaulting room of
an old chateau. We are quickly disabused of any notion that this is to be
just another gay party a la dolce vita. For also invited is a literal, by-
the-numbers, and intransigent prosecutor named Bitos whom they all
detest. He is to them the reincarnation of Robespierre; and through a
change of coats and the dramatic legerdermain of Anouilh the party
recreates the time of Robespierre and the French Revolution before returning to the humiliating harshness of the present. "Never' has Anouilh
exposed mankind with such caustic candor; and the device by which he
accomplishes this is a bitter and brilliant tragic-comedy."—*N.Y. World-
Telegram & Sun.* "He reminds us that man is unchangingly erring,
flawed man. Theatrical mastery. He weaves reality and make-believe into
a subtle web that intensifies the reality."—*N.Y. Times.*

(Royalty, $50-$25.)

IN WHITE AMERICA

By MARTIN B. DUBERMAN

HISTORY

3 black (2 male, 1 female)—3 white (2 male, 1 female)
Platform stage; musical interludes

An enactment from the actual records in the United States by a history
professor, this is the continuously absorbing story of the black from slave-
trade times to Little Rock. Winner of the Vernon-Rice-Drama Desk
Award. Here in a very gem of a letter are revealed the heart and soul of
a runaway slave in reply to a master who has asked him to return. Here
is the mournful account of a molested, widowed woman, and of her
crippled baby, and the Ku Klux Klan. Here, too, is the moving speech
by a southern senator in justification of lynching, the zenith of eloquent
emotionalism. Altogether, a beautifully arranged enactment, with scenes
of tremendous emotional power that will long endure.

(Royalty, $35-$25.)

DON'T DRINK THE WATER

By WOODY ALLEN

FARCE
12 men, 4 women—Interior

A CASCADE OF COMEDY FROM ONE OF OUR FUNNIEST CO-MEDIANS, and a solid hit on Broadway, this affair takes place inside an American embassy behind the Iron Curtain. An American tourist, caterer by trade, and his family of wife and daughter rush into the embassy two steps ahead of the police, who suspect them of spying and picture-taking. But it's not much of a refuge, for the ambassador is absent and his son, now in charge, has been expelled from a dozen countries and the whole continent of Africa. Nevertheless, they carefully and frantically plot their escape, and the ambassador's son and the caterer's daughter even have time to fall in love. "Because Mr. Allen is a working comedian himself, a number of the lines are perfectly agreeable . . . and there's quite a delectable bit of business laid out by the author and manically elaborated by the actor. . . . The gag is pleasantly outrageous and impeccably performed."—*N. Y. Times.* "Moved the audience to great laughter. . . . Allen's imagination is daffy, his sense of the ridiculous is keen and gags snap, crackle and pop."—*N. Y. Daily News.* "It's filled with funny lines. . . . A master of bright and hilarious dialogue."—*N. Y. Post.*

(Royalty, $50-$25,)

THE ODD COUPLE

By NEIL SIMON

COMEDY
6 men, 2 women—Interior

NEIL SIMON'S THIRD SUCCESS in a row begins with a group of the boys assembled for cards in the apartment of a divorced fellow, and if the mess of the place is any indication, it's no wonder that his wife left him. Late to arrive is another fellow who, they learn, has just been separated from his wife. Since he is very meticulous and tense, they fear he might commit suicide, and so go about locking all the windows. When he arrives, he is scarcely allowed to go to the bathroom alone. As life would have it, the slob bachelor and the meticulous fellow decide to bunk together—with hilarious results. The patterns of their own disastrous marriages begin to reappear in this arrangement; and so this too must end. "The richest comedy Simon has written and purest gold for any theatregoer. . . . This glorious play."—*N. Y. World-Telegram & Sun.* "His skill is not only great but constantly growing. . . . There is scarcely a moment that is not hilarious."—*N. Y. Times.*

(Royalty, $50-$35.)

THE MIRACLE WORKER
By WILLIAM GIBSON

DRAMA—3 ACTS
7 men, 7 women—Unit set

This stirring dramatization of the real-life story of Helen Keller is one of the most successful and warmly admired plays of the modern stage. Helen Keller was of course born blind and mute, and nobody knows what her ultimate fate might have been had she not providentially come under the care and tutelage of Annie Sullivan, the Irish girl who had been born blind herself and who was reluctantly hired by the agonized parents of the unfortunate little girl. *The Miracle Worker* is principally concerned with the emotional relationship between the lonely teacher and her blind charge. Little Helen, trapped in her own secret world, is bitter, violent, spoiled and, at first, almost animal-like. Only Annie realizes that there is a mind waiting to be rescued from the dark, tortured silence. Annie's eventual success with Helen comes only after some of the most turbulent, violent and emotion-packed scenes ever presented on the stage.

(Royalty, $50-$25.)

GOOD MORNING, MISS DOVE
By WILLIAM McCLEERY
from the novel by
FRANCES G. PATTON

COMEDY-DRAMA—3 ACTS
12 men, 10 women, extras—6 insets

This famous novel about a beloved school teacher has been expertly wrought into a funny, touching play by the celebrated author of *"Parlor Story," "Good Housekeeping"* and other popular comedies. Miss Dove is a school teacher who exercises great influence on the whole town of Liberty Hall. Graduates come back to her for advice. Everyone calls on her at the hospital during an illness. But the richest parents in town bring her before the School Board on charges of undue severity with their son. Helen Hayes starred in a 3-week production of *Good Morning, Miss Dove* at Catholic University in Washington, D. C.
"Sentimental, but never hazardously, thanks to Miss Hayes' crisp control and McCleery's flair for amusing insights . . . Reminiscent of Thornton Wilder's 'Our Town' . . . For all her firm, simple outline, Miss Dove is a complex character."—*Washington Evening Star.* "I like this play. I adore this character. I feel strongly about what this play says. . . . It is moving and exhilarating. Miss Dove, like Victoria Regina, does her job as she sees it."—Helen Hayes quoted in *The Washington Post.*

(Royalty, $35-$25.)

Come Blow Your Horn

By NEIL SIMON

COMEDY

3 men, 4 women—Interior

This fresh and delightful comedy was the surprise hit of the recent New York season. Harry Baker, owner of the largest artificial fruit business in the east, is the father of two sons. One is a 33-year-old playboy; the other a different, 21-year-old with an urge to assert himself. These two are continually trying their father's easily abused patience. Alan works only two days a week and goes on skiing or golfing jaunts with attractive female companions the other five. Buddy, hitherto an obedient son who even kissed Aunt Gussie through her veil at Dad's request, has moved into Alan's apartment, leaving a rebellious letter by way of explanation. The richly comic complications that ensue are unfailingly inventive and arise out of character, are never mere gags. "A slick, lively, funny comedy."—*N. Y. Times.* "It's completely nuts and banging with laughs."—*N. Y. World-Telegram & Sun.* "Warm-hearted and amusing."—*N. Y. Daily News.*

(Royalty, $50-$25.)

A Thousand Clowns

By HERB GARDNER

COMEDY

4 men, 1 woman, 1 boy 12 years old—2 interiors

Having created America's funniest creatures, the Nebishes, Herb Gardner turned his sights on Broadway and created the funniest play of the season, with "A Thousand Clowns." Jason Robards, Jr., opened in the role of a bachelor uncle who had been left to rear his precocious nephew. He has tired of writing cheap comedy for a children's television program, and now finds himself unemployed. But he also finds he has the free time to saunter through New York and do everything he has always wanted—like standing on Park Avenue in the dawn's early light and hollering, "All right, all you rich people: everybody out in the street for volleyball." This is not the right upbringing for a boy, however, and so a social service team comes to investigate him. Soon, however, he is solving their problems for them. He has to go back to work, or lose his nephew. Then on the other hand, he might even marry the girl social worker. The only thing we're certain of is that he will always be a cheerful non-conformist of the first rank.

(Royalty, $50-$25.)

A RAISIN IN THE SUN

By LORRAINE HANSBERRY

DRAMA

7 men, 3 women, 1 child—Interior

A Negro family is cramped in a flat on the south side of Chicago. They are a widow, her son (a chauffeur), his wife, his sister, and his little boy. The widow is expecting a $10,000 insurance settlement on her husband's death, and her son is constantly begging her to give him the money so that he can become co-owner of a liquor store. He wants to quit chauffeuring, to become a business man, and to be able to leave his son a little bit more than his own father, a brick-layer, had left him: this is the only way a Negro can continue to improve his lot. The widow, meantime, has placed a down-payment on a house where they can have sunlight, and be rid of roaches. The despair of the young husband is intense. His mother reluctantly turns over the remaining $6500 to him, as head of the house. He invests in the liquor store, his partner absconds, and his dream is forever dead. A representative from the better (white) neighborhood, into which they planned to move, calls on them and offers to reimburse them handsomely for their investment. But our young man now realizes that a little bit of dignity is all he can ever count on, and he plans to move his family to the new house.

(Royalty, $50-$25.)

PURLIE VICTORIOUS

By OSSIE DAVIS

COMEDY

6 men, 3 women—Exterior, 2 comp.

By taking all the cliches of plays, about the lovable old south and the love that existed between white masters and colored slaves, Ossie Davis has compounded a constantly comic play. Purlie Victorious has come back to his shabby cabin to announce that he will reacquire the local church and ring the freedom bell. There is an inheritance due to a colored cousin, which would be sufficient to buy the church, but unfortunately it also is controlled by the white-head plantation colonel. Purlie Victorious tries to send a newcomer to the colonel to impersonate the heiress, not only is she found out, but the colonel makes a pass at her. Eventually the church is recovered, services are again held in it, and the freedom bell rings. It is the dialogue, though, that makes the events so uproarious ("Are you trying to get non-violent with me, boy?") or human ("Oh, child, being colored can be a lot of fun when they ain't nobody looking"). There's uncommonly good sense in such a line as the one delivered to Purlie when he was about to beat the colonel with the colonel's well-worn bullwhip: "You can't do wrong just because it's right."

(Royalty, $50-$25.)

SPOON RIVER ANTHOLOGY

CHARLES AIDMAN

Conceived from EDGAR LEE MASTERS'
'Spoon River Anthology'

3 men, 2 women—A stage

Via musical interludes, we are introduced in a cemetery to the ghosts of those who were inhabitants of this town, and whose secrets have gone with them to the grave. There are 60-odd characterizations and vignettes in this constantly interesting entertainment, offering an amazingly varied array of roles and impersonations, from young lovers and preachers and teachers, to the funny chronicle of the poor mixed-up Jew who ends up in the wrong cemetery. Both the sordid and the humorous sides of life are portrayed, with fetching ballads, and the free verse form of Masters. "A dramatic presentation reduced to its simplest terms . . . moving and beautiful . . . an evening of astonishing stirring emotional satisfaction."—*N. Y. Post.* "A glowing theatre experience . . . a brooding and loving American folk poem brought to life on a stage."—*N. Y. Times.* "Vivid . . . quite an inspiration. . . . A decided novelty. . . . It has punch and humor and bitterness, and often it stabs the heart."—*N. Y. Daily News.* "Warm, radiant, poetic. . . . A compelling experience in the theatre."— *N. Y. Journal-American.* "A procession of unforgettable men and women, and a powerful evocation of life."—*N. Y. World-Telegram & Sun.*

(Royalty, $50-$25.)

DAVID and LISA

By JAMES REACH

Adapted from the book by THEODORE ISAAC RUBIN, and the screenplay by ELEANOR PERRY

11 men, 11 women

The production is extremely simple; it is played against drapes and uses a minimum of props. The award-winning motion picture, *David and Lisa,* has now been adapted for the stage with the utmost fidelity to its illustrious prototype. It retells, by use of the most modern stage techniques, the strange, appealing and utterly fascinating story of the two mentally-disturbed adolescents: David, only son of wealthy parents, over-protected by a dominating mother, who is tortured by his mania against being touched; and Lisa, the waif who has never known parental love, who has developed a split personality and is in effect two different girls, one of whom will speak only in childish rhymes and insists upon being spoken to in the same manner. The play follows them during the course of one term at Berkley School, where they have come under the sympathetic and understanding guidance of psychiatrist Alan Swinford and his staff; follows them through exhilarating progress and depressing retrogression; follows them—and their fellow students: Carlos, the street urchin; the over-romantic Kate; stout Sandra, and others—with laughter and heartbreak and suspense.

(Royalty, $35-$25.)

BUSY SPEAKER'S
POCKET PRACTICE BOOK

(Revised and enlarged)

By Belle Cumming Kennedy and Patricia Challgren. A foreword by Wilton L. Haverson, M.D., Dr. P.H. Diagrams and illustrations by Robert W. Teeter. A concise manual of tested exercises for voice and speech improvement prepared for public speakers, actors, clergymen, students and teachers. Written for those who are prepared to give a few minutes every day to the building of music, power and clarity into speech. It provides material for at least the first year of voice and speech practice. This is not a text book. It is a practice book, made to fit your hand, to lie flat on the desk, to stand upon a shelf. Spiral binding.

PRACTICAL AID FOR THE
INEXPERIENCED SPEAKER

By Belle Cumming Kennedy. A handy, quick-reference aid for anyone who wants to present his best personal appearance as a speaker before any type of audience. There are many methods and techniques presented in these twelve short lessons, all designed to give to the inexperienced speaker an understanding of the art of holding an audience. Among the lessons are: Developing Your Confidence; Planning Your Speech; Style; Platform Delivery; Introducing Speakers; and Points of Etiquette. A companion manual to The Busy Speaker's Pocket Practice Book. Spiral binding.

HERE'S HOW

A Basic Stagecraft Book

THOROUGHLY REVISED
AND ENLARGED

by HERBERT V. HAKE

COVERING 59 topics on the essentials of stagecraft (13 of them brand new). *Here's How* meets a very real need in the educational theater. It gives to directors and others concerned with the technical aspects of play production a complete and graphic explanation of ways of handling fundamental stagecraft problems.

The book is exceptional on several counts. It not only treats every topic thoroughly, but does so in an easy-to-read style every layman can understand. Most important, it is prepared in such a way that for every topic there is a facing page of illustrations (original drawings and photographs)—thus giving the reader a complete graphic presentation of the topic along with the textual description of the topic.

Because of the large type, the large size of the pages (9″ x 12″), and the flexible metal binding, *Here's How* will lie flat when opened and can be laid on a workbench for a director to read while in a *standing* position.

BOOKS ON THE THEATRE
REFERENCE POINT
By Arthur Hopkins

Having brought to our stage new methods of production as simple as they were revolutionary, Mr. Hopkins in *Reference Point* recapitulates personal theories, practices and conclusions on stage direction and production. It is a theatre book based on a series of papers read by Arthur Hopkins at the 1947 Theatre Seminar at Fordham University for drama teachers, directors and students from all parts of the country. It is best termed a book of practical idealism, for it is concerned with creative ways in writing, acting, and directing, and access to their source. "I want to stand up and cheer . . . Mr. Hopkins combed his memories, reflected on his principles and came up with some mighty sound, helpful and even inspiring comment." —Harry Hansen, *N. Y. World-Telegram.*

MODERN ACTING: A MANUAL
By Sophie Rosenstein, Larrae A. Haydon, Wilbur Sparrow.

The fundamentals of acting as taught at the University of Washington are compressed clearly and usefully in these pages. The approach and method are described and illustrated so that others may adopt them and profit by them.

PROBLEM PROJECTS IN ACTING
By Katherine Kester

Here are thirty scenes, varying from two to twelve minutes, which are so arranged that each scene appears as a complete unit and not as an excerpt from a longer work. The problem-project method is to emphasize the one important problem in a scene, and at the same time to correlate all the other factors involved in acting.

THE ACTOR CREATES
By Aristide D'Angelo, M.A., LL.B., instructor at the American Academy of Dramatics Arts.

This book originally intended for the use of students at the American Academy of Dramatic Arts, is addressed to actors, directors, teachers, and to that larger audience interested in the appreciation of play presentation.